REST IF YOU MUST, BUT

DON'T
YOU
QUIT!

ISBN: 978-1-937918-90-3

Published by:
Laurenzana Press
PO Box 1220
Melrose, FL 32666 USA

www.LaurenzanaPress.com

REST IF YOU MUST BUT

DON'T

YOU

QUIT!

Vic Johnson

& Champions From Around The World

*For my parents, John and Martha Scott, who
instilled in me the principle of persistence,
which dramatically altered my life in ways
unimaginable at the time.*

- Vic Johnson

Table of Contents

Don't Quit

When things go wrong as they sometimes will,
When the road you're trudging seems all uphill,
When the funds are low and the debts are high
And you want to smile, but you have to sigh.
When care is pressing you down a bit -
Rest, if you must, but don't you quit.

Life is queer with its twists and turns,
As everyone of us sometimes learns,
And many a fellow turns about
When he might have won had he stuck it out.
Don't give up though the pace seems slow -
You may succeed with another blow.

Often the goal is nearer than
It seems to a faint and faltering man;
Often the struggler has given up
When he might have captured the victor's cup;
And he learned too late when the night came down
How close he was to the golden crown.

Success is failure turned inside out---
The silver tint of the clouds of doubt,
And you never can tell how close you are,
It may be near when it seems afar;
So stick to the fight when you're hardest hit -
It's when things seem worst that you must not quit.

~ Anonymous

Introduction

Rest If You Must, But Don't You Quit!
By Vic Johnson

"Persistence and determination alone are omnipotent. The slogan 'Press On' has solved and always will solve the problems of the human race."

~ Calvin Coolidge

The poem on the preceding page was given to me more than forty years ago by a new friend, Mike Dunaway. It was framed, and I kept it in a prominent position on my desk or credenza for years. To this day I carry the poem on a card in my wallet. I can't think of a single significant accomplishment in my life that didn't require the commitment that its words command. Every single big achievement in my life would NOT have occurred had it not been for persistence.

Now there are times in life when quitting makes sense. Maybe you need to abandon a bad investment, or ditch an old garden because you're going to move to the city. Maybe you need to rest up a bit at the end of a tough day's work so you aren't too sore tomorrow.

But when it comes to the deepest dreams of your heart's desire — no, it doesn't make sense.

Don't quit.

Calvin Coolidge was on to something when he pointed out that talent and education had far less to do with success than most people thought. Coolidge, something of a self-made man himself, understood that talent and education only get you so far — when, in fact, quitting will rob you of all of the benefits of your "head start."

There is only *one* true human superpower we possess. It's not the power of flight. It certainly isn't the power of invincibility — anyone who's ever failed can tell you that!

It's determination. The ability to press on when you are tempted to quit. That is the one and only superpower you will ever have.

And the good news is that it's free.

It's just not easy. Especially when the world around you doesn't seem like it wants to accommodate your determination — which, let's be honest, is most of the time.

And because quitting sometimes *does* make sense (such as stopping a workout after an injury), how can you tell whether or not it's really time to give up?

We'll answer that question. But first, let's take a look at what the simple formula of determination can do for you.

The Postman Who Built a Palace

There's an old saying: how were the Pyramids built? Brick by brick.

A postman in France understood the truth of this axiom. Joseph-Ferdinand Cheval, a man who worked as a mail carrier in the French countryside in the late 19th and early 20th century, had a lot of walking to do. As much as 20 miles most days. This gave him a lot of time to think about his life and his dreams.

One day he started collecting stones he picked up during his walks. In fact, he picked up so many stones on such a regular basis that he eventually wore out the pockets of his pants and had to start bringing a bucket with him on his mail route.

His addiction grew and grew. Over time, the bucket wasn't enough. He wanted to carry bigger stones. So he started taking a wheelbarrow with him.

Over thirty years later, he had a palace on his hands. He called it Palais Idéal.

You see, Cheval and his wife put the stones to work, spending tireless hours building something of a palace.

Imagine that: building a palace by yourself without having to pay a penny for construction — or for materials. All it took was consistency and time.

Think for a moment of the great film, *The Shawshank Redemption*, when the character of Andy tunnels out slowly to escape his unjust prison sentence. How does he do it? Certainly not all at once; that would arouse suspicion. No; Andy instead smuggled handfuls of stones at a time, hidden in his pockets, and discreetly disposed of them in the recreation yard each day.

There is no limit to what you can achieve when you get the considerable resource of time working for you rather than against you.

For example, what if you had decided to write just two hundred words per day over the last year?

You would be sitting on top of a novel by now. Two hundred words per day — that's far less than what you've already read to get to this point. Two long paragraphs. Several short ones.

That's all.

But how often do we really channel our inner Cheval and get time working for us and not against us?

Take some time to think about what *you* could achieve if you were to invest a small amount of your resources into something new every day.

Consider what *you* could achieve if you picked up a few stones every day, as Cheval did.

Look around you. Where are the opportunities? It might seem as if there are none.

The truth is, you have to make your own opportunities. And if it seems like that will be too difficult a task to handle, then you've got to get out your chisel and start whittling away — a handful of stones at a time.

Don't Give Up Before You Find Your Gold

Of course, picking up a handful of stones one day and then dropping them the next won't get you anywhere. It's not the motivation that keeps you moving forward — sometimes, it's merely the discipline to keep moving ahead, even when the world seems like it's against you.

Consider the famous example in Napoleon Hill's *Think and Grow Rich*. In that book, Hill described the uncle of R.U. Darby, a man who moved out west to find a fortune in gold mining. If ever there was a less predictable, speculative venture as digging and *hoping* to find gold, I don't know it.

Darby's uncle did strike gold — a bit of gold ore that formed the foundation for some heavy equipment that would bring the gold to the surface and make them both rich!

There was just one problem. The gold ran out — rather quickly.

Darby and his uncle kept looking for more gold, on and on, until finally they lost their nerve and decided to cut their losses. The amount of money they invested in equipment turned out to be too much for them — so they finally called it quits and gave up.

They sold the equipment to a "junk man," who hired an expert to examine the area and see if the equipment might be of further use.

The expert determined that, yes, not only was there more gold — but there was more gold *just feet away from where Darby and his uncle had quit.*

If ever there was a story that demonstrated the power of persistence — and the helplessness of quitting — it's this one.

Napoleon Hill went on to point out that persistence was a trait shared by many of the great men and women he studied over the years. What many people interpreted to be "cold-heartedness" or "ruthlessness" was really just the learned habit of what Calvin Coolidge might call determination: the ability to see things through no matter what.

If Darby and his uncle had had this determination, this never-ending drive to succeed, they would have struck gold.

What is the area in *your* life that you've been putting off? The area that you've lost hope about due to lack of results? What part of *your* life could benefit from a little more persistence?

There's the old axiom that the definition of insanity is to try something over and over again and expect the same result. And to some extent, that's true. You shouldn't expect for your fortunes to change simply because you keep repeating the same action.

But true persistence allows for adaptation. It says, "I may change my strategy, but the goal remains the same."

That's not the definition of insanity. That's the definition of determination.

Sometimes, Persistence Alone is Enough

You might not think that persistence alone is enough. And maybe it isn't. In the film *Rudy*, the main character suffers from a complete lack of talent and athletic ability — and while his persistence wins him his dream of playing on the field for Notre Dame, his short stature ensures that that's as high as he'll ever reach.

But don't forget about the magic of persistence *alone*.

Consider the example of Cha Sa-soon, a woman from the small village of Sinchon in South Korea. Although she always wanted to drive, she never really started the process of learning to drive until she was in her sixties — well beyond what many people would consider a great time to start.

But it's never too late to start.

That was the case for Cha Sa-soon, who decided that it was time to drive. Armed with little driver's education but plenty of determination, she set about learning to drive.

And she failed. Not once. Not twice. Not thrice. She failed, over and over again... **949 times.**

How many of us wouldn't even get to 15 before we decided that maybe driving wasn't for us?

Because Cha Sa-soon was from a remote village in the mountains and had little concept of what driving was or how it might honestly be executed, she had no leg to stand on with these tests. In fact, she had no driving skills at all. But she was armed with that single, magical weapon of *persistence*. And in some cases, that's enough.

Persistence was magical enough in Cha Sa-soon's case that 950 attempts in, she finally passed her written test. Then came the actual driving portion of the test — which she failed only *four* times.

Imagine that: failing *four times* and having so much confidence that it seems like the *easy part*.

Eventually, the media got hold of Cha Sa-soon's story and made her into something of a local star. She starred in a Kia Soul commercial and was even awarded a car for her efforts.

Cha Sa-soon had everything going against her. She didn't have driver's education. She didn't have a history of driving. She didn't even have much of a rudimentary understanding of how driving works — at least not at the start. But through sheer will and determination alone, she didn't only pass her driving test. She became famous for it.

How many of us are willing to expend that amount of energy toward something even more substantial, like achieving our dreams?

If Cha Sa-soon can work that hard just to acquire her driver's license, why do *we* give up on our dreams after the first few rejections?

The answer is that we shouldn't.

In this book, you'll learn the difference between smart quitting — when it's a good idea to rest — and determination.

Determination, as Coolidge pointed out, is far more than just a decision. Determination is a decision that you don't make with your mind but rather with your soul. Determination is a decision that comes with a promise: that you will make something happen, come what may.

Cha Sa-soon decided that she wanted to get her driver's license. But it was no ordinary decision.

She *determined* that it would be so.

What will *you* determine?

Don't Quit: How to Cultivate the Energy to Persist in the Face of All Obstacles

It doesn't take much energy to quit. All it really takes is that you succumb to the emotions of the moment and say, "That's it. I've had it. Life wins."

But the truth is, it doesn't take much energy to persist, either.

I know what you're thinking. "Really? It doesn't take much energy to persist? Then how am I supposed to keep applying for jobs when I've already received fifty rejections? How am I supposed to work and work and work with zero expectation of any payment or reward?"

You make a good point. But consider this:

There is a stark difference between taking a break and calling it quits.

This book will help you understand that difference.

In this book, you'll learn:

- **How to find the motivation to persist, even when things aren't going your way.** It's one thing to draw inspiration from a story once. It's another thing entirely to value persistence so much that you keep returning to the battlefield, day in and day out.

- **Create specific lessons for getting the most out of your life.** That means cultivating your inner sense of determination — trumping other aspects of your life like talent and education.

- **Lessons for getting the most from this book and translating it into real-world scenarios.** It's not enough to understand intellectually. You'll learn how to take the lessons you read and apply them to real life.

Determination is not just a decision — it is a vow you keep to yourself. And in this book, you'll learn how the simple cry of "Don't quit!" can be enough to change your life forever.

About the Author

Vic Johnson was totally unknown in the personal development field fifteen years ago. Since that time he's created some of the most popular personal development sites on the Internet. One of them, AsAManthinketh.net, has given away over 400,000 copies of James Allen's classic book.

An eight-time Amazon best-selling author, he's become an internationally known expert in goal achieving and hosted his own TV show, Goals 2 Go, on TSTN. He has become a powerful authority in the self-publishing field and has taught thousands how to publish their first book. His three-day weekend seminar events, Claim Your Power Now, attracted such icons as Bob Proctor, Jim Rohn, Denis Waitley and many others.

This success has come despite the fact that he and his family were evicted from their home twenty years ago and the next year his last automobile was repossessed. His story of redemption and victory has inspired subscribers from around the world as he has taught the powerful principles that created incredible wealth in his life and many others.

For a free copy of his best-selling book *How To Write A Book This Weekend, Even If You Flunked English Like I Did* go to http://EbookMentor.com

His websites include:

AsAManThinketh.net

Goals2Go.com

GettingRichWitheBooks.com

TheChampionsClub.org

MyDailyInsights.com

VicJohnson.com

ClaimYourPowerNow.com

Chapter One

Is There Life After A Death Sentence?

By Karen Johnson

"Dream as if you will live forever; live as if you will die today."

~ James Dean

"I know exactly what is wrong with you," the doctor said. "You have muscular dystrophy." Those words brought Lynn Stevens' world crashing in around her. At 22 years old, married for under a year and caring for a newborn baby while living over 500 miles away from her social support system, this was a cataclysmic pronouncement.

When Lynn received her bombshell diagnosis, the medical community didn't have the information it now has. Her doctor couldn't tell her which of the 40 types of MD she had. They didn't tell her that she had a 50 percent chance of passing the condition to her children. They couldn't even tell her the best course of treatment. On that particular day, though, it didn't matter that they couldn't tell her any of that, because Lynn never heard another word spoken during that appointment. The words "muscular dystrophy" screeched and spun in her head like a maniacal demon, ripping apart her dreams, hopes and aspirations. They screamed that she would never see her newborn go to kindergarten, dress up for prom and graduate from high school or get married. At the tender age of 22, Lynn had just received what she believed was a death sentence.

This was not Lynn's first confrontation with a calamitous situation. When she was merely thirteen her father, always a cold and terse taskmaster, suffered a bout of post-traumatic stress disorder (PTSD). During his outburst, he attacked and seriously wounded a supervisor, resulting in the loss of his job and with it most of the household's income. Over the course of the following three years,

23

Lynn witnessed and experienced multiple instances of physical and verbal abuse. Her father's unmanaged rage, fueled by drugs and alcohol, manifested itself through attacks on her mother. These violent episodes were interspersed between periods of neglect, during which her parents would often disappear for days at a time, leaving Lynn to fend for herself while they partied. By the time she was sixteen, her parents had become so disengaged from her life that when she announced that she was moving out, they barely protested.

As Lynn progressed through the stages of grief that ultimately led to her acceptance of her circumstances, she became determined to make the most of her life. She was working on her bucket list long before the movie premiered. Lynn personified James Dean's admonition to "dream as if you will live forever; live as if you will die today." When asked what kept her going through difficult times (such as sleeping behind dumpsters after she left her parents' home, being arrested for shoplifting food when she didn't have enough money to eat, and being treated as invisible because she happened to be in a wheelchair), Lynn replied, "It never occurred to me to quit."

One of Lynn's lowest points came about three years after the diagnosis. Her husband was under pressure due to his schooling, and Lynn refused to deal with her condition. The combination of the school pressure and Lynn's denial of her disease took its toll on the relationship; the couple separated. Lynn soon found that she could not survive on the monthly disability payments she received. In order to care for her daughter, Lynn returned to work, despite her medical condition. When she first emancipated herself, she worked as a taco fryer. Now, as an adult, she worked as a regional manager specializing in trouble shooting and cleaning up "problem stores" in the Taco Bell chain. The pressures of the demanding job along with the strain of raising a toddler by herself exacerbated her symptoms. However, the worst was yet to come. Soon Lynn began to notice her daughter was showing signs of MD. Her heart was broken. Her worst nightmare was coming true.

The manifestation of her daughter's symptoms prompted Lynn and Aaron to resume communications. As they worked together to help their daughter, Lynn and Aaron fell back in love. When Aaron was sent by the Navy to Del Rio, Texas, Lynn decided to go with him.

Despite her own physical challenges, Lynn maintained her status as social butterfly and community volunteer. When tropical storm Charley wiped out the bridges connecting Del Rio to the rest of Texas, Lynn found she was the only Red Cross Volunteer stranded in a town that was two-thirds underwater. She was tasked by the Red Cross to be their "boots on the ground," assessing conditions and reporting them to the Red Cross headquarters.

The situation at Del Rio transformed the way Lynn saw life. She became keenly aware that a life can change at a moment's notice, often due to circumstances totally outside of a person's control. Most of the Del Rio residents went to bed that night completely unaware of the disaster that stalked them in the night. Lynn's focus changed. Money was no longer the biggest issue. She realized that money didn't matter; *life* mattered! She lost her desire to move up in the corporate world. That drive to succeed was replaced by a compulsion to make a difference in the community.

While Del Rio and Lynn continued their recovery from the storm, Aaron accepted a new position. With the new position came a move to Pendleton, Oregon. All during the moving process, Lynn was torn. Should she pursue a new job in the corporate world, or should she follow her heart and work in social services? While the money in the for-profit arena was nice, she was still haunted by the faces of the survivors in Del Rio searching for their loved ones. Lynn submitted applications for positions in for-profit companies, but when the time came to commit to interviews, she could not bring herself to go. She ultimately became the very first executive director of a not-for-profit children's museum in Pendleton.

During her tenure at the museum, Lynn became pregnant with her second child. As with her first pregnancy, her MD symptoms went into overdrive. Also, the possibility that this child, like her daughter, had a 50 percent chance of having muscular dystrophy became frighteningly real. While her daughter had outgrown the early symptoms, Lynn still lived with the possibility that they could return at any time. What did this mean for the small life growing within her? It meant that he would receive steroid shots in utero to prepare him for an early delivery. It meant that Lynn spent a month in the hospital on complete bed rest in a city a long three-hour drive from everyone she knew. It meant that when labor was induced, Lynn's bed was surrounded by experts from the neonatal unit. They were so ready to handle the emergencies that go along with the birth of a four-pound baby that they were almost disappointed when he emerged perfectly normal and healthy.

At least he seemed healthy. The truth did not reveal itself until three days later, when Lynn made a horrifying discovery.

Gazing at the already winged scapula of her precious son, Lynn knew instantly and without a doubt that he had MD. Crushed, Lynn thought, "I did this to him." Again, Lynn grieved, this time for Colin. Again, as with every challenge presented to her before, Lynn refused to let this tragedy stop her. She kept moving forward. She told herself, "I got through the tough stuff before; I can get through this, too." Giving up was not an option. Lynn committed herself to perseverance.

Soon Lynn and Aaron found themselves in North Webster, Indiana where a community group to spearhead efforts to raise money to save the community's old high school from being bulldozed recruited Lynn. This venerable historic building held a special place in the hearts of most of the area's residents, as they and their parents and their grandparents had graduated from there. Lynn got things done, and as a result, she was recognized by various groups with awards such as "Person of the Year," "Lady of the Year," "Chamber Member of the Year," "Lioness Person of the Year," just to name a few. Today the community center is a self-sufficient, thriving monument to Lynn's commitment to improve the lives of the people in her community.

Lynn loved living in North Webster. Not only was she close to their extended families, the town was small; there were only about 400 full-time residents. While this made North Webster a charming place to live, it also presented problems. Lynn received all those awards, but she also received attention that was not quite so flattering. Meddling town members spread rumors suggesting that Lynn's many social interactions were not all for the benefit of the community center. These tales eventually took a toll on Lynn and Aaron, and for a second time they separated, this time remaining apart for over two years.

As Lynn worked two jobs to support herself and the children, she grew increasingly unhappy that her children were forced, through no fault of their own, to live in a broken family. Both she and Aaron had grown up in two-parent families, and Lynn was angry that small-town gossip had robbed her children of a stable, intact home. Lynn decided that giving up on her marriage was not an option. After a series of excruciating conversations, Lynn and Aaron put the children's best interests first and decided to move their family back together, away from the small town that had ripped them apart.

Lynn and her family ultimately moved to Shreveport, Louisiana. Shreveport was big enough to minimize the effect of small town gossip and had enough warm weather to soothe the physical pain Lynn endured each day since MD took a toll on her muscles. While in between jobs in the non-profit sector of their new city, Lynn invited her parents for a visit. Over the years, she had come to forgive them for their shortcomings as parents and wanted her children to have a relationship with them. On Thanksgiving Day, as the visit was nearing its end, Lynn took her father to the VA hospital to treat what she thought was a cold that had developed into pneumonia. They were stunned to learn that the condition was actually lung cancer. Two weeks later, her usually stalwart mother cut short an outing because she didn't feel well. Her trip to the doctor revealed that she had a collapsed lung. Suddenly Lynn found herself caring for the parents who had failed to make a home for her. True to her innate character, Lynn decided that turning them away was not an option.

Today Lynn lives with her husband, her children and her parents. She continues to serve her family and community, all while coping with the complications of muscular dystrophy. She has suffered through several serious falls that resulted in positional vertigo and ultimately prompted her to succumb to the full-time use of a wheelchair. She cares for her mother, who suffers from dementia, and her father, who wrestles with PTSD. She worries about her daughter, who has opted not to be tested for MD, and her son, who is working on fulfilling his own bucket list, knowing that a future of facing challenges from MD looms before him. She also works full-time as the Chief Operations Officer of the United Way of Northwest Louisiana.

Lynn now tells people that the day she was diagnosed with muscular dystrophy was the best day of her life. Why? It made her decide that she would live her life with passion, never taking tomorrow for granted. Since being diagnosed with the life-robbing condition of muscular dystrophy, Lynn has driven a race car at 165 mph, gone whitewater rafting in the Grand Canyon, swam with sharks and has tackled life head on with determination few people develop. Her bucket list includes traveling to exotic locations before MD steals that joy from her. Quitting is still not an option!

Don't let personal challenges become an excuse; you can accomplish great things. When faced with the unfair situations life hurls at you, pull yourself up to meet the challenge. Don't succumb to grief and despair. Hold your head high and give it everything you have. I challenge you to make your own bucket list. Refuse to allow giving in or giving up to ever become an option.

Dream HUGE, and get started living those dreams today.

About the Author

Karen Johnson is a mentor for passionate business owners and executives. By combining her extensive business experience with a proven methodology she delivers a coaching program that covers every aspect of the business, including leadership, people management, and exit strategies. The result is increased profits and cash flow, and a stronger, more accountable team.

For more information on how to engage Karen to be your coach, go to www.fpcoachla.com. She can also be reached at karen@YourExecutive.Solutions

Karen also authored *Business is a Battlefield: Tales from the Trenches*, where she shares other real stories of real people in the business world.

Chapter Two

You're Fired. You're Fat. You're Screwed!
By Gregory Oliver, D.O.

"You have two primary choices in life: to accept conditions as they exist or accept responsibility for changing them."

~ Denis Waitley

I'm a doctor, but at the time of this story, I was a patient. As I quietly lay on the operating table while nurses, technicians and other doctors prepped me for an 8-hour heart procedure, my thoughts began to race. They were about to rewire my heart to correct a dangerous rhythm pattern. I had been in these operating theaters hundreds of times, but I had always been on the other side of the table. I knew the machines and equipment, but I had never had them attached to me.

Much as I tried not to dwell on the negative, I couldn't help but to acknowledge the risk inherent in undergoing surgery. I had seen patients die while undergoing procedures just like this one. No, my entire life did not flash before my eyes as they initiated the anesthesia, but I certainly did think about my life. The good, the bad and the ugly.

I've decided to tell you about the ugly.

We all encounter ugly things and bad times. What we do with them determines who and what we become. Not unlike you, I have endured crappy times, but I want to tell you about three specific experiences that changed the course of my life. These ugly times taught me valuable lessons and turned out to be blessings that directed me on a path toward my dreams.

You're Fired!

I'd always wanted to be a doctor, ever since the fifth grade. I worked hard to that end and graduated college with very high grades and test scores, and yet I was denied admission to medical school. Heartbroken and sitting in my dorm room looking out the window (tears streaming down my cheeks), I decided I was not willing to give up on my dream. Instead, I sought advice from both a physician mentor and the medical school dean. They gave me direction, and I did exactly what they told me to do. I worked hard and slept little during the coming months, but I was accepted into the medical school of my choice the following year. I continued to exhibit this same level of diligence and persistence throughout medical school and graduated third in my class. I was happy to have proved the first admission committee wrong. I obviously belonged in medical school.

After medical school and residency, I joined a small family medical practice where I worked 60 to 70 hours per week. After 18 months, I had built a large practice, generating 10 times my salary. I felt I deserved a raise. However, when I asked the practice owners for an increase, I was not just told no. I was told, "You're fired!"

"Fired? Seriously? After working my butt off to grow your practice?"

As I looked across the table at the two doctors who were firing me, my initial reaction was to strangle them. That thought quickly dissipated, morphing into red-faced, blood vessel pumping anger that would soon drive me to perform at an even higher level. As I left the practice, I embraced a new purpose: I would prove these people wrong.

Now with a wife, two sons and bills to pay, I was without a job. A sinking feeling overcame me as I feared that I would not be able to provide for my family. I grabbed hold of the intense anger within and determined to move forward quickly. Within 72 hours I'd found a small house with an abandoned medical office on the first floor and sent letters to several hundred people. I saw my first patient in my new office the following week. I became my own receptionist, nurse, doctor and financial manager. My initial income was meager, so I took on a part-time job working the emergency room from 9 p.m. to 9 a.m. two nights a week. I worked at my office 9:30 a.m. to 7 p.m. each day. I refused to let fatigue get in my way. The income from the emergency room kept me afloat. I kept thinking, "I will show up those jerks that fired me by building a practice bigger and better than theirs." I realized later they didn't care and probably never even thought about me, but this worked for me. I used my anger to motivate me in positive advancement of my goals.

I knew I could be successful on my own, so I developed a plan to buy a medical building and expand my practice. I asked my banker for a loan, but I was turned down. Banks don't care if you're nice or a hard worker; they want to know how you're going to pay them back, and I didn't have sufficient proof to show them what I was capable of doing. Again, as I was turned down, I felt anger bubbling up inside me, and again, I channeled it into productive action.

I asked the banker for advice on getting a loan. He gave me suggestions, and I followed them to the letter. I went to 21 banks and was rejected by 20. With each no, I felt down and unworthy, but after each rejection I asked the banker delivering that awful news for more advice on getting a loan. Each banker gave me suggestions, and I acted on the advice I was given every time. By the time I approached the 21st bank, I had compiled an impressive package of documents, design plans, references and details proving my practice was a worthy investment. That 21st banker offered me $400,000 to start a family medical and urgent care practice. Over the following five years I built five family medical/urgent care centers and hired 15 doctors to work for me. Asking for help, learning lessons from each rejection and being persistent paid off. Each time I was told I couldn't, I did! I never let rejection get me down. Instead, I became determined to prove each of the previous bankers wrong.

You're Fat!

I had always been physically fit, but focusing on my career and my family found me 50 pounds overweight. One day upon entering the exam room of my long-time patient Natalie, she looked me in the eye and said, "Doc, you're fat!" She was right. I felt embarrassed and mad at myself, but she was right. I spent the rest of the day irritated, like the tag of a tight shirt collar was scratching me.

I decided to face the truth: I was not a good example for my family or patients. I was frustrated with myself, but instead of giving up, I used the negative emotions to motivate me. I studied obesity, and I developed a plan to lose weight, improve my health and become an example of health again. Over the next three months, I lost 45 pounds and discovered renewed energy.

After keeping the weight off for a long time, life threw me another curve ball: I developed a heart rhythm disturbance that left me tired, weak and unable to exercise. My cardiologist put me on medications, but these just exhausted me. To my chagrin, I gained back all the weight I had lost.

For a short while, I threw myself a few pity parties and allowed myself to feel more like one of my sick patients than their doctor. However, I soon realized this depressed feeling wasn't getting me anywhere, and I decided to undergo the heart surgery, risky and inconvenient as it was. My energy returned within a few months of recovery, and I felt 20 years younger and ready to move forward.

I restarted my weight loss plan and worked hard to shrink back to my lean weight. As a physician, I felt obligated to also help my patients lose weight and become healthy, not just treat them with medicine to control obesity-related disorders. I derived great satisfaction from helping my patients beat their weight problems, and as a result, I started a second medical practice for the treatment of obesity. Using the dietary plan and nutrition and exercise counselors that had helped me get results, I turned my own struggles with my weight into a thriving practice. Since its inception, we have helped thousands of patients lose weight, reduce dependency on medications and live their lives more fully.

The lesson to be learned? Life's journey has obstacles. Find a way around, over, under or through them. Turn frustration into victory.

You're Screwed!

As time passed, my hard work and persistence paid off financially. I had established successful medical and weight management practices, and I realized I should be proactive with my assets. I joined an investor mentoring club that boasted a quality education program and reputable mentoring system to learn real estate investing. The club was in Los Angeles, and as I lived in Indianapolis, I flew to L.A. each month for the meetings. If I was going to learn, I wanted to learn from the best. The program taught me valuable and important skills, and I soon began to invest in various real estate projects.

Along the way I met new friends, fellow investors and other experts in various fields of finance. One of these educators owned a company that invested in high quality assets and had produced strong investment returns for over 20 years. After a couple of years of studying his investment program and meeting other long-term investors in his fund, my wife and I invested a large portion of our retirement savings into this plan.

Shortly thereafter, unusual things began to happen. I stopped receiving statements. Upon contacting the company owner, I was assured that everything was fine and this was just a "glitch." Soon after this, the SEC and FBI shut down the company and confiscated all of the assets. Attorneys, FBI agents, SEC agents and receivers became involved.

Long story short, I was told, "You're screwed!" Your funds are gone.

We were out $750,000.00 thanks to this Ponzi scheme. The moment I was told "you're screwed," I felt nauseated. I had worked so long and hard to put this money aside for my future and now it was all gone.

I was angry. Depressed. I couldn't trust anyone. How could someone I knew and trusted have such disregard for my investment?

The nausea persisted for months, hitting me even as I tried to pour myself into my patients and my practice. At times I would close myself off in an exam room and brace myself as I endured an irrepressible flood of rage, tears and anxiety. What was I going to do now? How could I replace our retirement savings? Would I ever be able to work and live life with a smile on my face again? I wanted to exact vengeance.

I was too embarrassed to share this with anyone. However, after months of going through the motions, I realized something incredibly important. I was still alive. My family was intact. Aside from the loss of money (which I wouldn't need for several years), I was okay. I needed to get it together and move forward faster than ever.

This setback required the biggest attitude adjustment of my life. I had to completely change my thinking so I could recover. Through this loss, I discovered that I was the only person in control of my future and I was responsible for everything in my life. It was time to prove once again that I would not be held back — not even by thieves.

You're in Charge!
Facing the ugly events of our lives drags up unwanted emotions, but it is necessary if you want to move forward. Before you take

one more step toward pursuing your dreams, I ask you to heed my hard-learned message.

First off, you must accept the fact that life *will* throw crap at you. That's a given. It happens at the most inopportune times. It can sneak up on you or hit fast from out of the blue. Sometimes misfortune is of our own doing, and sometimes we suffer because someone else has his or her own agenda and does not care how it affects you.

When it happens, whatever it is, you will ride an emotional rollercoaster. Like me, you will feel angry and embarrassed. You will ask, "Why me?" It's okay to cry, yell, hide in bed or have a pity party, but you'd better restrict the time spent in the *poor little ol' me* zone.

After you've processed the emotions of the experience, take action! It's your responsibility to catch the crap that has been flung at you. Analyze the ugly event. Get advice from a mentor who is dispassionate about the outcome.

When you've explored the entire spectrum of the worst and best case scenarios, you must dispose of the crap. Don't let it defeat you! Instead, grab the reigns and harness the emotions. Let the pain motivate you to do better. Prove the naysayers wrong.

Most importantly, you must remember: you control your own destiny. The wisdom and character gained from these adversities will help you grow into the most amazing version of yourself possible.

About the Author

Gregory Oliver, D.O. is a practicing family physician, whose passion is helping people live the healthiest quality of life possible. His initial writings were four manuals to assist his patients to reduce weight, improve fitness, and reach optimal health. Dr. Oliver's *recently* published books are *I Just Can't Lose Weight – Seven Reasons Why and How to Beat Them* and *Lean on Me – Your Journey to Forever Thin*. Dr. Oliver believes strongly in personal development and shares self-improvement lessons with family, friends, co-workers, and future doctors. His goal is to help each person he encounters to live life to the fullest.

Email: fatdocthindoc@gmail.com
Website: fastclinicalweightloss.com

Chapter Three

It's Never Too Late to Be What You Might Have Been

By Daryl A. Zipp

"It's Never Too Late to Be What You Might Have Been."

~ George Eliot

Has there ever been a time in your life when you've taken a good look at yourself and been terribly disappointed with what you saw? I'm talking about a complete, sober estimation of everything in your life — your situation, your lifestyle, your source and amount of income, your health, your weight, where you live — everything? If you're anything like me, I'm sure you have. At many times, I wasn't happy with my life, but each time I persevered through change. One of my favorite quotes is credited to the 19th century author, George Eliot: "It's never too late to be what you might have been." Take a minute and think about the implications of what the author is saying. This doesn't only apply to me; it applies to anyone whose life plans have been interrupted by … well … by life. This is my story.

My dad died when I was three years old, and my mom was left to raise us alone while also working a 9-to-5 job to support my three sisters and me. She was an incredibly loyal and hard worker, and she never called in sick. This worked well for me because mom was never home until evening, so when I was in high school, I could skip out of class and come home any time I wanted to. As I'm writing this, my mom is taking a nap on the couch in front of me. She's 95 years old, and I'm blessed to still have her with me.

I was one of those guys in high school that allowed the other two-thirds of the students in my class to graduate above me. I couldn't be bothered with homework; no sir, not me, I had better things to do after school, like play football at the park. I was smart enough to pass the tests. I did pay a little attention in class, but I was the guy that pretty much went to school just to find out where the parties were on the weekend.

Graduation came and went, and then I was out on my own doing what everyone else was doing — I got a job and spent time punching a time clock. I worked at a book bindery where I put book covers on books and put books in boxes — all day long. I did this, day in and day out. My goal was the same as everyone else's, just make it to Friday — pay day. It was so boring that I soon quit.

I then went to work for a construction company where we built commercial buildings. I was earning three times minimum wage; none of my friends were making this kind of income. At first I thought I had it made, but boy was I wrong. The job called for working outside in the Texas heat in the summer. Many days it was over 100 degrees. It wasn't exciting work and was very physically demanding on my body.

This was the time that I made my first very important career decision. Even though I was making good money, I decided it was time to walk away from the mental and physical anguish of hard manual labor. I evaluated my needs and determined that I wanted to find a better way of making a living, doing something that I would actually enjoy. With no other prospects of income in sight, I quit my construction job and decided to go back to school to study computer science at a local college. At least that was the plan — life sometimes has a way of forcing a change of plans on you — and the unexpected happened.

I wanted to work part-time while attending college, so I searched the newspaper for jobs each day. One day, I found an ad that read "Horse Drawn Carriage Driver Needed to Give Tours in Downtown

San Antonio, TX. I thought, "Wow, how cool would that be?" But I just let it pass and didn't take it seriously. Two hours later, I was sitting outside with my mother having coffee when I heard a horse walking down our street. I went out front to take a look and there it was: a horse pulling a fancy carriage. I checked the name of the company, and sure enough, it was the same as the ad! What were the odds of this? In the entire 24 years I'd lived there, I had never seen a horse come down our street. I thought this was a message from Jesus. I checked out the opportunity, and since I was the only guy that showed up for the job, I was hired.

Since the owner of this carriage business was investing most of her funds into a new restaurant, the carriage business suffered. The horses were old and were unable to work more than a few days a week. My work schedule shrank, and my earning potential shrank along with it. However, I loved driving the carriages, and I didn't want to find other work. I thought outside of the box, and that's when it occurred to me that I could buy a horse and carriage and start my own horse drawn carriage business.

I looked into what that would require, and I was told I needed to make a presentation to the San Antonio city council at their open meeting. Public speaking terrified me at the time, but my vision of starting my own carriage business spurred me on. As I faced the nerve-racking ordeal of public speaking, my goals (and the reasons behind them) became clearer to me; I wanted to work on my terms, doing something I was passionate about, and enjoying the freedom of a business owner.

Understanding the reasons behind my goal helped me push past my fear. It wasn't that the fear of public speaking disappeared, but rather I found the strength to overcome it. Sure, my presentation was disorganized, and I was definitely not the most polished speaker, but I did it. The city council appeared to view me as a nuisance, and I was told that the advisory board would contact me after they studied the impact of my proposed business on the city, but still I went home satisfied. I had done my best.

About two weeks later while in the checkout line at the grocery store, I heard someone say, "You're Mr. Zipp, right?" I was very surprised to see it was Mrs. Helen Dutmer, one of the ladies from the city council meeting. Mrs. Dutmer was a businesswoman, and she liked the horse drawn carriages. She told me not to wait on the city council because it might take a few years before they are able to get to us. She said that there are no laws or city ordinances to prohibit my business. She told me to keep those carriages out there; they are a popular attraction and are good for city tourism.

That day I walked into the grocery store to get beer and sausage, and I walked out of there in the horse drawn carriage business. This is a testament to the power of honoring your desires and vision. When you take action steps towards a worthy goal and have faith that it can work, things fall into place. I so desperately wanted to raise my standard of living by creating my own successful business. To put some fun and freedom in my life like I never had before. Was luck involved? Maybe so, but none of this would have happened if I had not pushed past my fear and embraced the determination I needed to make it happen.

Soon after opening in San Antonio, I also opened up a carriage business in Houston, TX. Then in Galveston Island, TX. After that, I went to New England and opened up a carriage business in Boston, MA. A born-and-bred Southern boy, working in the Northeast. Now that was a culture shock!

Life was good for quite a while; I operated my carriage business for 21 years. I had made a great living. I could travel whenever I wanted. I owned a very large home, with a barn and riding ring. My carriage business had grown to be more than just tours of downtown areas; I now drove a lot of famous individuals in my horse and carriage. I did a TV commercial with our former ex-governor of Texas, Mr. John Connally, who was very excited to drive my team of Clydesdales. I was on national television with the Perry Como Christmas Show. I had Perry Como, Angie Dickinson and George Straight in my carriage. We did a birthday party for the wife of Steven Tyler, lead singer of the band Aerosmith. I had Julia Roberts in my carriage at the National Hockey League Party. I even held the Stanley Cup on the coachman seat of my carriage — now, that was pretty cool, it's also a memory that will last forever.

However, my success did not last forever. As often happens in life, I hit an obstacle that was out of my control. On August 6, 1997 while driving my horse named Chief in Boston, I was on my way to pick up a bride and groom from a wedding at the Old North Church in the historic North End. That's when a large commercial truck struck us from behind. The force of the collision threw me out of the carriage into the middle of the street, breaking both of my ankles on impact. Chief lay in the street with a bloody broken leg.

Chief died that day, and that was the beginning of the end of my carriage business. I was unable to train my horses or to drive a carriage or even stand on my feet for any length of time. In the following two years, I underwent several surgeries — hospital stays. I had six pins in each ankle, casts, wheelchairs, crutches — the list goes on and on. I became depressed. I lost my passion, and as a result I also lost my vision for the business. I reluctantly sold my business and returned to San Antonio without any plans for the future.

Here I was, 46 years old and wondering how I was going to support myself. I had made a very good living with my carriage business. Negativity flooded me; all I could think was that I would never find something as good as my carriage business. What was I going to do now? Bills piled up. My problems multiplied.

At long last, I had a breakthrough. You see, I had rested for a while, but I never truly quit. My broken ankles healed, and now it was time to start my emotional healing. I made a decision to get out there, push through the fear and pain and create my own income again. I spent time thinking about how much I had enjoyed running my carriage business and decided to trust that I could start a new business, something that would be just as lucrative, flexible and rewarding.

Then I took those important first steps. I beat the streets of San Antonio, actually knocking on doors, looking for homes that I could buy, rehab and resell for a profit. I did a few transactions and realized I liked the industry enough to work for and get my real estate sales license. The money was nothing compared to what I was making in my previous business, but I had found my way out of the darkness of depression. I was on my way back up.

I let the frustrations I felt about my low income motivate me to take more action steps. I explored options, looking for the perfect opportunity that would suit my skill set. That's when I discovered the world of real estate brokerage.

I had already learned that leverage works wonders. You see, as an agent, my income was dependent on my sales record. However, as a broker I benefit financially from the sales of multiple agents. I would be able to work less and make more money; how appealing, right?

I studied hard and jumped through all the hoops required by the Texas Real Estate Commission, and then I took a leap of faith — I started my own full-service real estate brokerage company. Texas Premier Realty now has offices throughout Texas, with over 250 agents in our brokerage, and still growing. Life is very good. I am making an income of over four times what I made in my horse drawn carriage business. I feel very blessed.

My story reads: rags to riches, back to rags and then to more riches. Through it all, I learned that the main ingredient to success is personal growth. God gave us natural talent and ability; we just need to take the initiative to develop that talent. If you allow limiting beliefs to dominate your thinking, you will not succeed. I personally believe that the Devil uses doubt and fear to limit us, but God can help you break through those limitations. If you have faith in your heart, fear and doubt will flee.

My most important tip to you is to create a lifestyle vision and then work strategic plans that serve that vision. If you do not succeed at first, you did not fail — you just need to make a better plan. The journey may be long, life may throw obstacles in your way, but you can make it if you just keep at it.

Rest if you must, but do not quit — your happiness and your legacy depends on it.

About the Author

Born and raised in Texas, **Daryl A. Zipp** is an author, entrepreneur, and real estate broker. He is also the founder and owner of Texas Premier Realty, a firm with 250 agents — and growing. Daryl was in an untimely accident that began a two-year ordeal of surgeries and rehab, forcing him to change his lifestyle and his way of making an income. Daryl believes that it's possible for anyone to change the direction of any part of their life. He shares the story of his beginnings to his success, to his crippling accident, and then back to beginnings and success again. You can contact Daryl at dzipp@satx.rr.com.

Chapter Four

Treasure In The Sea

By Kimberly Schmidtke

"Never give up, for that is just the place and time that the tide will turn."

~ Harriet Beecher Stowe

As I sit in my home office preparing to share my story with you, I can't help but reflect on how amazing my life is. I woke up this morning, like most mornings, without an alarm clock blaring. I woke up naturally because I had slept as long as my body needed to rest.

After drinking a leisurely cup of coffee and eating a light breakfast, I went for a power walk. I love my daily walks through the beautiful woods that surround my neighborhood, located just outside Seattle, Washington. It's a great way to start my day.

My three sons are all out of the nest now and pursuing their own dreams. I love having the freedom to spend time with them and not having to ask a boss for time off.

The "Never Quit" Attitude

My mother and father gave me (and my brothers) a lot of love as we were growing up. One of the ways they showed me their love was by pushing me and helping me understand what it would take to be successful. In particular, my dad taught me that it was essential to persevere and never quit. He had lost his father at a young age and didn't have the money for college, so he worked hard and won a scholarship. He passed along that work ethic to me.

But he didn't just tell me to work hard. He also taught me to believe in myself and to trust that I had the ability to achieve my goals. He would often say to me, "You are destined for greatness, but you're going to have to pay the price. Success doesn't happen overnight. There are going to be times that you might not feel like doing something, but it will be worth it if you just consistently keep trying."

I attended college at the University of Washington and the University of Colorado. Upon graduation, I worked in corporate sales. I loved my jobs, but when my first child was born, I left corporate America to be a stay-at-home mom.

Home May Be Where the Heart Is, But You Need Income, Too

When my sons got older, I started working in network marketing to supplement my income. I was just hoping to make a couple thousand dollars a month. I loved the concept that this sort of work would allow me to create a residual income while remaining in control of my schedule.

As my father predicted, I was not an overnight success. I struggled to make sufficient money through my first two network marketing efforts. I made a lot of friends, but not enough income. I was passionate about what I was doing and I worked hard, but I just couldn't get any traction.

Although I ended up quitting those two businesses, I still liked the concept of network marketing. I also realized that the time I spent working in those businesses wasn't a total loss. I learned a lot and grew as a person. They just weren't the right vehicles for me. They didn't have a system in place to help me replicate my success, so I was limited in my capacity for growth and income.

Then a friend told me about Nerium. At first, I wasn't interested. My first two experiences made me hesitate, but deep inside I knew that I could be successful at network marketing, so I looked into this particular opportunity with a keen eye. Could I take a different approach with this company and make it work?

I could see that my friend was passionate about the company and their product. And, when she told me that the company was only eight months old, I saw the tremendous value of getting in on the ground floor.

I reminded myself that all I had was the present moment, so I seized the opportunity and didn't look back. I became laser-focused and worked as hard as I possibly could.

Our Ship Comes In, but Then is Shipwrecked

The company took off very quickly, and by the time I had been in about two years, they had grossed about $400M in sales. I was very excited about the prospects. I became even more excited when I heard that we were scheduled to open in Mexico. I had a team leader that was from Mexico and I knew that she could build an organization.

Sure enough, we were successful. My team and I quickly built organizations in 14 states in Mexico. The team grew to 368 members. We continued to work fervently to expand the team before the launch. We were having fun and making a lot of memories. We knew that it was a special time in the business.

We were poised for success, but the launch was delayed, and seemingly as fast as we had built the Mexico team, it disintegrated. It was so sad to watch it happen and not be able to stop it. The leader of the group in Mexico was very distraught and confessed that she was tempted to quit.

I told her that she was an amazing leader and that she had no idea how many lives she was going to impact if she persevered. I kept the dream in front of her by reminding her that she would be able to spend more time in Mexico, her native country.

I also repeated to her some of the things my dad had said to me as I was growing up.

"I believe in you."

"You are destined for greatness."

"You are a champion."

I told her, "Let go of the work we did. No matter what, we're not going to quit — no matter what." I told her that maybe this happened for a reason, but whatever the case, quitting was not an option. This became our mantra.

We Put our Boots Back On, and Our Business Skyrocketed

To boost our morale, we both went on a company-sponsored incentive trip to Cancun. My Mexico leader stayed an extra day after I went home; little did she know how important that extra day would be — for her life, and for the lives of many others. On that last day, she decided to go for a swim in the ocean, and while swimming she met a family from Monterey, Mexico.

After working up the courage, she started talking to them about our business opportunity. She told them that the company would soon open in Mexico and encouraged them to go to the opening ceremony. Two of the family members did and ended up joining our team.

The new Mexico team grew rapidly under the leadership of the Monterey team. That growth helped propel me to the position of Three-Star National Marketing Director, as well as helping me win bonuses of $50,000 and $150,000. Talk about sweet success!

When You Are Tempted to Quit

Someone recently asked me what my biggest challenge is and what I do when a team member wants to quit. My answers were simple.

My biggest challenge is the "naysayers" — you know, the people who say you can't do it. The challenge is too great; the odds are against you; the stakes are too high. Naysayers are everywhere, and we all have to choose how we will respond to their very loud, very negative voices.

I've learned to deal with their negativity by just blocking it out.

No matter what you do in life, there will always be people who will tell you that it won't work. They just can't see the vision. Maybe they've been beat up a lot and they just can't see the possibilities. Maybe the timing is not right for them. Maybe it will be right later, though.

I think one of the biggest difficulties is that people want success to happen overnight and it doesn't. You've got to stick with the program. You've got to do the work. You've got to stay consistent. My experience is that the small victories build upon each other. For me, it's a little win, after a little win, after a little win. Eventually, all those small victories thread together and lead up to a big win.

Most people expect to receive too much in the way of rewards in too short of a period of time. I believe that (as Bill Gates says) "most people overestimate what they can do in one year and underestimate what they can do in ten years."

When a person on my team struggles, I tell them that quitting is not an option. Then I suggest that we look at what we need to change to make the business work for them. I tell them to stay plugged into the system and to the events because they need the support and to learn from the people who have figured out how to make it work. I let them know that I believe in them. I don't just say this: I truly keep believing in them until they can believe in themselves.

I remind them that I took a leap of faith when I decided to join my third network marketing company. I share that I was scared, too, but it worked for me because I stuck with it and I figured out what was required to get the lifestyle I desired. I love freedom. I love being able to do whatever I want, whenever I want. I love waking up when I'm done sleeping.

Most of all, I love residual income. I feel so secure because I know that income is going to come in and in, over and over and over and over. It is kind of like having 10 rental properties that are all paid off. Through my business, I feel like I've got 21 or 22 amazing rental properties that are all paid off and the checks just keep coming in every month because the properties are rented out. I always knew about residual income, but boy when you have finally built up a business that truly delivers, it really is a beautiful thing.

I also tell them that they need to immerse themselves into personal development. I tell them to lock arms with the positive people in their life. I remind them that they really are the average of the five people that you spend the most time with.

When you invest in personal development, you are investing in your ability to keep moving forward. You can do this in many ways, but I personally prefer conferences and seminars. I recently attended a seminar featuring Brian Tracy and have booked an upcoming seminar with Darren Hardy that I'm excited about attending. Hopefully, I'll be able to get to Tony Robbins and Eric Worre seminars soon as well.

It's important to build a positive shield around yourself. As Zig Ziglar said, "People often say that motivation doesn't last. Well, neither does bathing — that's why we recommend it daily."

What If I Had Quit?

Today, I have teams in Canada, US, Mexico, Japan and Korea. We're about to launch teams in Australia, Hong Kong and Colombia. I was recently inducted into the Million Dollar Club. I've won hundreds of thousands of dollars in cash bonuses and a Lexus car, not to mention all of the expensive bonus trips I've been on. The future looks bright.

None of that would have been possible if we had quit after losing the first Mexico team.

You see, treasure really does exist. It's buried somewhere in the ocean. If you take the time to search for it and surround yourself with people who know how to find it, you can and will find it for yourself. It simply takes time and guidance from people who have gone before you.

As I finish telling you my story, I'll leave you with a final thought: If you are tempted to give up, I encourage you to "rest if you must, but don't you quit." Keep going and you'll find your "treasure in the sea."

About the Author

Kimberly Schmidtke was born in Portland, Oregon in 1961. She received her degree from the University of Washington and resides presently in Snoqualmie, Washington. She is the mother of three grown boys, Calvin, Barrett, and Tucker. She loves spending time with them as well as building her global business and traveling the world with her family and friends. Kimberly is a Three Star National Marketing Director with Nerium International, which is a Billion Dollar Company, and she is a top earner and is in the Millionaire Club.

Email: kimmerthecat@hotmail.com
www.kaglobal.nerium.com
Cell   253-514-9846

Chapter Five

Jock To Jackpot!

By Ray Morey

"Formal education will make you a living; self-education will make you a fortune."

~ Jim Rohn

I grew up on the wrong side of town — the other side of the tracks on the north side of Tulsa, Oklahoma. As far as I was concerned, we were rich. We were rich spiritually and rich in family. I don't remember ever lacking food or clothes to wear.

My mom was 16 when my brother was born. Two years later, when I came along, our parents were already separated and the three of us lived with my grandmother until our mom remarried (when I was two). As a young child, I had a lisp and didn't like to talk. My older brother, Ronnie, spoke for me whenever possible so I wouldn't be the subject of ridicule. In addition to having a lisp, I broke 200 pounds in sixth grade. You get the picture, right? I was the shy fat kid that constantly got picked on and was in fights almost every week.

It wasn't until ninth grade that I realized we were not financially rich. At 14, I grew into my body, becoming a decent football player at 6'1", 215 pounds. I was recruited to play football for a south-side private Catholic high school. To this day, I still remember my first time visiting that school. The long tree-lined drive and beautifully manicured lawn looked like the entrance to a university. As we toured the facilities, I was amazed at every turn. The hallways were clean and the windows did not have cracks. The kids wore uniforms and were well behaved. Some of them looked at me funny, but nobody seemed threatening.

Do you know what they had in their weight room at this high school? Weights. Yeah, they actually had weights and weight machines… something I had never seen before. The coach talked about how they traveled to Texas and Arkansas for games. Needless to say, I was impressed — and excited! I remember sitting in the coach's office while he spoke with my parents. I already had my future planned out. I could do three years here, then on to the University of Oklahoma, and then the pros. Woo-hoo... what an opportunity!

Then reality came crashing down.

Realizing the Truth

I don't remember the exact price they quoted, just that it was too high. There was no money in the family budget for private school. No way, out of the question! That was the day I realized we were not rich financially.

Fortunately, I ended up going to a great public high school. It proved to be best for me, and I met my future wife there. We married when I was 19; today we have two wonderful children together and recently celebrated 34 years of marriage.

While I always enjoyed football, I suffered two knee injuries that kept me from pursuing the sport beyond high school. After graduation, I got my first real full-time job working in a factory that made seals for the oil industry, and I faced the reality of working for the next 50 years — most likely as a machine operator or manual laborer.

That's just the way it was in my family. No one went to college. They joined the military or they worked, usually more than one job at a time, just to make ends meet.

Trying Something Different

Just because you recognize the truth doesn't mean you can't take action to better your situation. You may need to work harder than someone born with an easier lot in life, but it doesn't mean you are doomed. You just may have to try something new. That's what I did when I found myself daunted by the future that loomed before me.

I was 18 when a co-worker introduced me to network marketing. I liked the idea of doing something different and earning extra money. From the age of 18 to 33, I joined several network marketing companies and experienced varying degrees of failure.

Most of the companies are still in business today and many people have had great success and made lots of money, so it's fair to say it wasn't those companies that failed; it was me. At least that's what I thought at the time — that I had failed. It wasn't until recently, looking back on these experiences, that I understood how much I was actually learning along the way. I didn't fail. Sure, if I'd given up, that would have been failure. What I did was learn and grow, and over time, I built valuable skills and knowledge that I use each and every day.

To my surprise, the opportunities in my full-time jobs during this time greatly increased. I originally thought I would always be a blue collar, labor-type person. I worked as a tack welder, machine operator, meter reader and various other types of labor positions. But ironically, as I got involved with network marketing, I began to develop new skills that carried over into other parts of my life.

The first company I ever joined sold health supplements. Through that experience, I learned how to handle rejection. Do you know that rejection doesn't actually cause physical pain and you can move forward after it? That realization prepared me for my future career in sales and helped me learn to ask, "What's the worst that can happen?" I found out that someone telling me "no" wasn't the end of the world.

The second company I joined offered legal insurance and was actually the first of its kind. My time with that company taught me to give presentations. I learned how to talk to people. At the time, I was interviewing for a different position at work, and I remember facing the interview with a confidence I hadn't previously possessed. I got that job and was actually one of the youngest ever hired into that position.

For my full-time job, I worked in customer service at a public utility company. After a couple of years, I noticed that they didn't have a serious collections department for old invoices. I asked if I could pursue this, was given permission, and went on to develop the paperwork and procedures for this new department. Again, learning to handle rejection paid off in my new venture in more ways than one.

Because of our success, the company decided to create an actual collections department. Unfortunately, they then found a person with a college degree to run it and then filled all of the openings with people with college degrees. This really devastated me at the time; I felt like a failure. However, I now see that I learned valuable skills that have served me well.

Never Stop Learning

Ironically, another position opened up at one of the power plants, so I found myself back in overalls, working in the labor field. At this time, I joined another network marketing company in the insurance industry. The process to get licensed was not easy and required me to become a real student. I studied hard and passed the state insurance test on my first attempt.

This was one of the best lessons I ever learned: how to study. I also realized I wasn't a dumb jock. I learned I could do more than just manual labor. I began to believe I could do more than I had previously thought possible.

Another thing I learned is there is a 92 percent failure rate in the insurance industry. Unfortunately, I fell into that category.

In 1985, the power plant shut down and, once again, I was looking for a job. I became a route salesman for a uniform rental company, but after several months of working this position, I decided I needed to go back to school. If I hadn't studied for and passed the licensing exam, I might have thought I could not handle school, but that experience helped me see that I could take it a step further, and I was soon in school to become a computer programmer.

I didn't actually end up working as a programmer, but I gained knowledge and confidence as I went to school. Instead, I was offered a job in sales, which went quite well for me. I excelled at my job and was promoted to sales manager. The business changed hands, and I was sent on international business trips to Taiwan.

I was assured that my lack of a college degree would not hamper my future development. Still, I couldn't help but notice that all the new employees, including the receptionist, had degrees. It wasn't long after that I was asked to move from my corner office to down the hall, and then later to the absolute farthest office away from the boss. Then he asked me to travel three weeks per month, which I wasn't willing to do. I had young children at home; I couldn't bear to be apart from them three-quarters of the time.

I left the position, but I took the lessons I had learned with me. I was a capable sales representative who could handle international business trips. I was a scholar who could pick up a new skill. I was smart and capable; these were important lessons for me to learn.

Peeking Behind the Curtain

It was then that I joined a network marketing company that offered long distance phone service at a competitive rate. From this experience I learned how to teach and motivate. I also learned to look behind the curtain and see that not all leadership has your best interest in mind.

At my full-time job, the new owner continued to staff the company with family, including three sons and his wife. I could tell my time there was limited. In 1996, we parted ways and I joined a startup network marketing company, but that also only lasted a few months.

After quitting my corporate job, I was trying everything I could to make money in network marketing, but finding nothing but dead ends. Because of that, I left the industry and swore I would never do it again. I still remember how devastated I felt facing the reality that I had to go find another job. In 1997, I began working at another company that was in the same industry I worked previously, the place where I still work today.

Still, in the back of my mind, I always knew that in the traditional business world I would be limited by my perceived lack of education. I had spent more than 25 years working in the seal and bearing industry, making good money, but I didn't have a degree to document my knowledge and the majority of my income was always dependent on oil prices.

With the desire to be the captain of my own ship and a keen awareness of what to look for before committing to a company, I decided to give network marketing one more try.

Taking Another Shot

In 2015, I was introduced to a company unlike anything I'd ever seen before. They provide essential services such as electricity, natural gas, mobile communications, virtual MD, roadside assistance, identity theft protection, to name a few, with more services coming in the future. I loved the fact that with this opportunity, I would be adding value to my customers' lives instead of asking them to buy an extra product that wasn't already in their budget.

This time around, though, I've studied the industry more than ever. By reading books, listening to CDs and audio books and attending every training seminar offered, I've learned more in one year than

I have in the last 15 or 20 years. I have also pursued my own personal development. It's a different time, a different company and I'm taking a different approach. But I'm also using all of my experiences from the past. Remember, these "failures" aren't really failures if you learn from them.

Reaping the Rewards of Lessons Learned

Today, I reflect back upon my life and wondering if I'm only just now putting the pieces of that puzzle together. I look back and wonder, "What if?" What if someone didn't ask me to join? What if I said no? The answer is that I wouldn't be where I am today.

My life today is so different! I have traveled to almost every state in the USA and to Canada, Germany, Austria, China and Taiwan. I've also enjoyed relaxing vacations to several islands in the Caribbean and Mexico.

My advice for anyone that wants to improve his or her lot in life is to make the decision to change. Step out of your comfort zone. As Vick Strizheus says, "Massive imperfect action is better than perfect inaction."

Do not worry about failing! You will fail at times because we *all* fail, but *you* can chose to fail your way to *success*. You may need to take breaks, and there may be times when you change course, but whatever you do, you must not quit!

About the Author

Ray Morey started out as an obese, shy boy with a speech impediment, barely graduated high school and faced a future of blue-collar jobs. In his early twenties he discovered the idea of "Self Improvement" while venturing into the world of network marketing. The lessons learned during these years were applied to his day job and he began to grow professionally and financially. In his early thirties he started investing in real estate and continues to oversee his properties. He is now considered in the top of his field in network marketing and continues to mentor.

RayMorey.com
r.morey@sbcglobal.net

Chapter Six

Quitting Is The Journey; It's Not The Destination

By Larry Thompson

"It takes courage to quit a job. It takes a fool to quit on yourself."

~ Larry Thompson

There are many iconic cities in the world — London, New York, Paris, Rome... and I have been fortunate enough to visit each and every one of them. But for me, the most important city in the world will always be El Paso, Texas. Needless to say it is not because of the fine dining, natural beauty or the fact that it is where Donald Trump wants to build a wall, but because El Paso is more than a location for me. It is the place where I had to make tough decisions. The place where I had to decide whether or not I believed in myself.

Humble Beginnings

Before I went to El Paso, I was a high school dropout and a long-haired hippie construction worker. It was our family business, and it was all I knew... until I met a man named Bobby Depew.

Bobby was working for a network marketing company that promoted more than just products. They also supported the idea that ordinary people could collectively work together to accomplish extraordinary things.

Bobby told me the company was going through a national expansion and I had a chance to be at the forefront of this incredible ground-floor opportunity. I didn't know it at that time, but that sales pitch is what every network marketer uses to recruit people, regardless of the scope of their "expansion plans" — to add one more distributor to their organization or expand to one more city. The company only had representatives in the San Francisco Bay Area at that time, so they were looking for distributors who would take on new cities.

I was excited. I could have chosen from any city anywhere on the planet, but for some inexplicable reason I heard myself saying, "I want El Paso."

Keep in mind, I had never been more than 45 miles from my hometown of Livermore, California, and three days later, I was in El Paso. I didn't know anyone in the entire state of Texas, never mind El Paso. All I had was Jim Rohn and Bobby Depew motivational tapes, a telephone and a long distance calling plan that was prohibitively expensive.

Sponsors didn't call anybody. The company didn't call anybody… least of all me!

My goal was to create a $100,000 worth of business in the next 90 days; my intention was to become a part of the corporate team. Bobby told me I could own this area, be responsible for this success story and have my name published across the country.

Bobby said the key to success was to have opportunity meetings followed by trainings on Tuesday nights, Thursday nights and Saturday mornings at the local hotels. I would be part of what they called the "co-op." Each of the top distributors would pony up $50.00 a month to the co-op to cover all the costs. That sounded great! However, when I got to El Paso as the sole distributor, I was, by default, the co-op. It never dawned on me I would be footing the entire bill until I could sign up another distributor. When I realized this, I responded with something I labeled "panic," but Bobby called "purposeful motivation."

The cheapest hotel I could find (where a guest would not be afraid to attend a meeting) was a Holiday Inn. The hotel would only rent me the meeting room for an entire month at a time at a cost of

$600.00 up front. To give perspective, the apartment I was staying at was only $200 a month. It was an investment, to say the least.

The First Meeting

Back then it was quite a project to put on a meeting because we didn't have an established brand. You had to have a projector, an impressive product display, a big registration table. All this cost money.

I quickly understood that until I signed up a distributor and started to build a team, I would have to carry the load of all of the responsibilities. It wasn't just a financial burden, but also a manpower challenge. I had to pay for the meeting room and the product display, but I also had to run the projector, register people, present to the audience and convince people to sign up after the meetings.

I didn't know how I was going to handle it all, but I did know I wanted my name published across the country. I didn't know where it was going to be published or who was going to read this publication, but I was convinced that that was the moment when I would have arrived!

I never will forget that first Tuesday night.

I set everything up. I had my shoes shined and put on my best suit. The product display looked great. I worked through the practical details of how to run the meeting. I was ready!

The meeting was scheduled to start at seven o'clock, but at 6:55 nobody was there. Seven o'clock came and went — still no one. 7:15, 7:20, 7:30... still nobody.

I don't know why I expected anybody to show up because I hadn't invited anyone!

It never occurred to me that I had to invite people. I knew I didn't invite anybody, but I still expected somebody to show up. After a couple of disappointing evenings, I realized that an advertisement in the local classifieds was far more effective than just hoping and waiting.

The ads were effective in getting people to contact me, but I still struggled to get people to sign up. I was puzzled. How did this work so well for Bobby but wasn't working for me?

I was scared of running out of money before I could find the right people with whom to collaborate, but I was strong in one area: I refused to let go of my belief system. To help me stay strong, Bobby sent me an audiotape he had recorded titled the "SINALOA" an acronym that stands for safety in numbers and law of average using the 10-Penny Method. It essentially said that the law of averages is as powerful and predictable as the law of attraction.

This is how SINALOA works: First thing in the morning, put 10 pennies into your left pocket in the morning. As you go through your day, move a penny to your right pocket every time you legitimately invite someone to look at your business and they answered "yes" or "no." Then refuse to go home until you've moved those 10 pennies into your right pocket.

I agreed with Bobby's principle. If I moved 10 pennies a day, I'd start getting people to my meetings. The hard work would start producing results. Little by little, I would move my business forward.

It took me at least another three weeks before I actually moved 10 pennies from my left pocket to my right pocket in a day. People started attending the meetings — two people, three people, six people — but still nobody joined.

Bobby also said that I would sign up approximately two out of ten people who attended the meetings. He said, "You get two out of ten. It's nothing but numbers."

He said that if you invite ten people, you will net two that show up. If you get ten to show up, you will net two that sign up. If you get ten to sign up, you will net two who start moving. If you get ten to start moving, you will net two that recruit other people.

The following week seven people had attended the meeting, but still nobody joined. Eleven people attended, but nobody joined. I told myself, "It's okay; the law of averages will catch up with me."

I had seventeen people attend, and yet no one joined. I was still the only one in the room doing the distributor role. I was paying for everything. I was doing all the work. I was the only one recruiting.

Then I had twenty-three who had attended and still nobody joined; it was getting very scary. My confidence was shaken and the clock was ticking. I was digging in to this 90-day timeframe and nothing was happening.

I had every reason in the world to quit — every single reason you can imagine.

I would call my wife every couple of days to get some positive reinforcement. She was scared to death. She wanted money to pay the car payment. She wanted money for this and that, but I didn't have it. She couldn't offer me support because she was justifiably terrified that this idea would put us under.

Thirty-two people to the meetings and still no one joined. I could feel the walls closing in. Forty-six people to the meeting, still no one joined.

I still can remember going to my room at night and waiting for that midnight hour. Wide awake lying there at ten minutes to midnight. Tears running down my face. The closer I got to midnight, the more relief I felt. Each night, as the clock struck midnight, I breathed a sigh of relief. I had made it through the day without quitting.

Next day, the 52nd person came to my meeting. Thus far, fifty-two people (in a row) had come to the meeting but turned me down.

Looking back on that time, I don't know why I didn't quit. Was it because I felt like I didn't have any place to go, or was it because I felt I was one step closer to where I knew I was going? Was it because I couldn't face my friends and family who said a salesman doesn't earn an honest living because they don't work with their hands?

It might have been because Jim Rohn said to me, "Don't wish it was easier; wish you were better. Don't wish for fewer problems; wish for more skills. Don't wish for less challenge; wish for more wisdom."

Number fifty-three

Then number fifty-three turned out to be Mark and Charlotte Parkhurst. Mark worked in the oil fields, and they were just regular everyday people.

And they said YES!

Not because my meeting or presentation was any better. Not because I learned a different technique or started to talk to different types of people.

They said yes… because SINALOA, safety in numbers and law of averages, is a principle proven to me that you can count on.

Over the next 30 days, I put over 50 people in the business, and I started making money. I made about $10,000 over the next 30 days. (That's $100,000 in today's dollars.)

I know you are thinking, "Man, Mark and Charlotte really must have been big hitters." Actually, they weren't. They were great people, but they were C-team players. They used to feed me, let me come over and play with their kids. They gave me some security. I now had some friends, and I also had some help at the meetings.

But the reason I had success was the fact that SINALOA is a principle that works and the numbers played out and it always does. It happened because I had a consistent effort, my attitude, confidence and passion waivered, but the reality of SINALOA carried me through.

And each and every day all the reasons to quit were still there, but I ignored them! All the signs were there that I should have quit; I didn't know there was a number 53 …that would change my life. I don't know what would have happened if 53 didn't show up, but he did. Good day or bad, I just put one foot in front of the other. One foot in front on number 50, number 51, number 52 and so on! And this taught me that in every difficult situation in life, or "El Paso Moment," there is always a 53 if you don't quit.

Throughout my entire career I have been back to El Paso many times… not to the city, but to the place where I encountered difficulties of life. I knew to overcome I simply needed to apply the principles of SINALOA by doing the right thing in a right manner consistently over a prolonged period of time. I needed to not quit and let SINALOA bring the next "53"!

My original El Paso moment was the foundation that allowed Mark Hughes and I to build Herbalife International into a $100 million-a-month, $1 billion-a-year company in less than five years. Herbalife has become a 4 billion dollar-a-year company that has positively impacted millions of people's lives throughout the world and has survived many "El Paso Moments."

In your life, El Paso moments will always find you, and there is always a 53. Put your stake in the ground, work hard until your 53 walks through that door, refuse to quit!

See you in El Paso, and let's have dinner with 53!

About the Author

Larry Thompson - Mentor to the Millionaires
www.larrythompsononline.com

- Named by The Wall Street Journal as "the Architect of Wealthbuilding"

- Over 50 years of experience in the Direct Sales/Network Marketing Industry

- Creator of Millionaire Training Concepts being taught globally

- Mentor and coach to top leaders and entrepreneurs around the world

- Historian and teacher of the history of direct sales industry and philosophy

- Mastermind of the success strategies of Herbalife International

Chapter Seven

The Power Of The Semicolon

By Robert Crockett

"Don't go around saying the world owes you a living. The world owes you nothing. It was here first."

~ Mark Twain

"Jack's dead!"

Those were the words I woke up to on a Sunday morning in February 2009. On the other end of the line was one of my caregivers, Lori. She was in a panic, unsure what she should do. Jack, a 29-year-old former bodybuilder suffering from bone cancer, had succumbed to the pain and debilitation caused by his cancer. He didn't die naturally. He parked his motorized wheelchair at the entrance to his apartment, tied his dog to the wheelchair and then took enough pain medication to cause his death.

Lori had been taking care of Jack for years; as such, they had developed a strong bond. Knowing how upset she was, I asked her to close the door to the apartment and wait outside while I called the police and made the drive over to Jack's apartment. After I called the police (still reeling from the phone call), I woke up my son, who was 14 at the time. I explained what happened and asked him to get dressed and come with me.

On the drive, my son was silent. We were both digesting what had happened. We had owned and ran a home care agency in Las Vegas since 2003. We weren't strangers to death — close to 200 of our elderly clients had passed away — but this was different.

This was Jack, one of the youngest people we cared for and the first client I allowed my son and daughter to get close to.

Jack loved big event movies, but due to his condition he couldn't go unless someone took him. I started taking Jack to movies he wanted to see and always brought along my kids so they could get real life exposure to how difficult some people's lives are. Jack never actually stayed awake for the whole movie; a lot of times his pain medication was so strong that he would fall asleep partway through the movie. There were even times he fell asleep during the coming attractions. When they were younger, my kids used to look on in amusement. They'd nudge me and whisper, "Jack fell asleep again." After a while, they realized it wasn't the movie itself that was important to Jack; it was the experience of being with us at the movie that was important. My children learned a great deal about patience, compassion and understanding just by being around Jack. Over the holidays, he would call and talk to my kids, wishing them Merry Christmas. Then I would get on the phone with him and he would tell me he loved me and he thought of me like a father. I loved him, too.

But now Jack was dead. Suicide. A person I cared for was in so much pain that he took his life. I didn't see it coming, or maybe I chose not to recognize the signs. It wouldn't be the last time I had this feeling.

After Lori finished her interview with the police, I sent her home and called Jack's mom (who lived 30 minutes away). I told her I was sorry to have to tell her that her son passed away, and we discussed the fact that someone needed to come claim Jack's possessions, including his dog. She told me she had a lot to do that morning and she would come over as soon as she was done with her errands. To this day, I don't know if she was in shock that her son had passed away or if she just didn't care.

After I got off the phone with Jack's mom, I told my son that we couldn't just leave Jack's body lying on the gurney unattended while the police and coroner finished their investigation and paperwork. We had Jack's dog to care for as well, so we sat on the curb outside Jack's apartment and talked.

We spent a few hours out on that curb, and during that time, we had an important conversation. I don't know if it was my Midwestern stoicism or the age of my son that had previously prevented me from opening up about things I had witnessed over the years, but that morning I started talking and told him things that I had never discussed with anyone else. I was terribly upset with myself for not recognizing Jack's despair and loneliness, so it's hard for me to remember the exact words we shared, but I know for certain that I spoke at length about how difficult it was to have clients die every month. I shared how much it saddened me to take care of people who lived in poverty and needed a lot more help than we could provide, and I explained that I kept doing it because I was confident that we provided more compassionate and higher quality care for these people than anyone else would.

Eventually the police and coroner finished up, and I said goodbye to Jack. We waited in the parking lot until everyone had left before we returned home, taking Jack's dog along with us. At some point the next day a friend of Jack's mom came over and picked up the dog. Nobody from his family ever asked about his suicide or questioned me about what caused him to take his own life.

Two years passed by, and although I thought about Jack often, I was determined to not make the same mistakes I made with Jack. To that end, I took a series of courses through the Jason Foundation on youth suicide prevention. Fortunately, life goes on, and eventually the emotions of that day subsided and I only remembered everything that was good about Jack. That is... until I received a series of texts from the parents of a friend of my son who were alarmed at some comments my son had made.

They were afraid he was going to hurt himself. As I read some of the comments my son had made, I felt the same sense of failure I felt when Jack died. How could my son be in so much pain? Why couldn't I see it?

I went to my son's room and asked him what was going on. At first he was adamant there wasn't a problem, but I didn't give up. It took a while, but he finally opened up. He started talking, pouring out everything he had bottled up. I was crushed at the depth of his pain and disappointed in myself for yet again not recognizing the fact that someone I loved was suffering.

After a lot of talking and much discussion about how to move forward, we were both drained. However, I didn't want to leave him by himself. I finally blurted out that I didn't want to leave because I was afraid he was going to hurt himself. He told me not to worry about it; he was past it. I told him I couldn't help but worry about it; I was his Dad, and I couldn't help being scared. We went back and forth a couple of more times, and he finally said, "Really, I'm past it. When I was at my lowest point, I heard your voice telling me 'If you remember one thing about today, promise me you'll remember that if you're ever alone and thinking about suicide, you need to realize that things may seem bad, but it will pass. You are going to have an incredible lifelong journey.' That's what you told me while we sat in front of Jack's house after he committed suicide."

I looked at my son, trying not to let my emotions get the best of me. I didn't remember saying that to him. I hugged him, grateful that this was what he remembered from that sad day. Then I told him I loved him and trusted him, and then I left his room so I could collect my thoughts and think about what had just happened. While I was shaken, frustrated and scared, I soon realized that I had just received a tremendous gift.

These two experiences changed me. I try to think before I speak now and make sure I've considered what the other person is going through; I also try to temper my tone so it isn't harsh. A couple of times I've slipped, but my daughter, who is 17 now, has reeled me in and put things in proper prospective each time. For example, one time we were watching a movie and a family a few rows from us were talking and laughing loudly. I whispered to my daughter that I was going to tell them to be quiet. She said, "What if they can't normally afford going to movies, and this was an important event for them? Would I feel bad if the moment they remembered from their special night was me scolding them?" Another time someone cut me off while driving and I started swearing. She said, "What if they just found out their kid got hurt and they're rushing to get to them? Wouldn't you drive as fast as you could to get to me?" I'm 38 years older than she is, but somehow she ended up with more wisdom.

Five years have passed since the conversation in my son's room. He's is an incredible young man on an incredible journey. We still provide care for the elderly and disabled, managing 200 caregivers who go from home to home providing service every single day. It's still a grind, and it can still be disheartening at times to realize these people deserve more help and support than we are able to provide. I think about Jack almost daily. I feel that I failed to help him, but out of that tragedy, my son gained a lifeline that I'll always be grateful for. Despite multiple offers to purchase my company, I'll never sell it and will never quit providing care to people who need it. It is my opportunity to make a difference; it is my way to honor Jack and teach my son to persevere.

When my son graduated high school and started college, he decided he wanted to get a tattoo that would have a lot of meaning to him. He decided to have a semicolon tattooed on the inside of his wrist. When he showed it to me, my first thought was that a semicolon tattoo seemed a little weak; I then asked him why it held so much meaning to him. He told me about a non-profit called Project Semicolon that encourages people to tattoo semicolons on their bodies as a way to support those who struggle with suicide. He then shared a quote posted on their website:

"A semicolon is used when an author could've ended a sentence but chose not to. You are the author and the sentence is your life."

I'm reminded of the power of that quote and how much I wish I could have helped Jack every time I think of my son.

From Jack's tragedy, I learned important life lessons that I wish I had learned decades sooner. One is what you say and the tone you use matters. It may not seem important to you, but you don't know who is listening and how they're interpreting the things you say. Sometimes kindness and patience is the greatest gift you can give someone.

The second is for people who are scared and feel alone and have thought about committing suicide or hurting yourself. You're not a bad or damaged person, and you're not alone! You can get through this hard time and go on to enjoy an incredible life! Talk to someone. If the first person you reach out to doesn't seem capable of hearing the things you need to say, talk to someone else. If you can't find the support you need from the people around you, there are incredible support groups in most areas and a wealth of information and support on the Internet. Rest if you must, but please don't quit. You need to keep going. Don't give up before the circumstances you are facing have a chance to improve. There are solutions, and your perseverance may help others after you.

Author note: The names of the caregiver and the client were changed to protect their privacy. If you're considering harming yourself or have thought of suicide and have nowhere else to turn, you can call the National Suicide Prevention Lifeline at 1-800-273-8255. Service is available to everyone, all calls are confidential and people are available to take your call 24 hours a day, 7 days a week.

About the Author

Robert Crockett is the proud father of two amazing children residing in Las Vegas, Nevada. He's been involved in numerous start-ups and turnarounds and currently operates Advanced Personal Care Solutions, a home health care company he founded in 2004 that has over 175 employees that provides support services to the elderly and disabled. He also works with other companies as a John Maxwell coach and speaker and a Gitomer Certified Advisor.

Email: Robert@rpcrockett.com

Web site: rpcrockett.com

Twitter: @RobertPCrockett

Chapter Eight

Walk It Off

By Mike Tobias

"Invest in as much of yourself as you can; you are your own biggest asset by far."

~ Warren Buffet

"I've lost my home and life savings of over a million dollars!

"Are you kidding me? This cannot be happening to me! There's got to be a way out. I refuse to believe there's not a way out. Come on! Think. Why is this happening to me? Have I really lost everything I've been saving for the last 20 years?"

The voices in my head were so loud that I'm not really sure if I just paced the floor or if I actually said the words out loud.

As a serial entrepreneur, I had taken calculated risks before. Some have worked and some haven't, but I didn't see this failure coming. It wasn't supposed to be so risky that I might lose everything, and yet it was, and it happened. This investment was supposed to pay out in dividends; I was going to use the profits to pay for my dream home, in cash. The plan backfired, and there was nothing I could do about it.

After 20 years of working hard and saving my money I had finally reached my goal: a bank balance of over $1 million. Not bad for a latchkey kid on the free lunch program, raised by a single mom. I was so proud of the self-discipline I had practiced and the fact that I had actually met such a lofty goal. I'd set a goal and by the grace of God I finally achieved it. Only my wife and my banker knew I'd made it happen because I wasn't an overnight success; it's not like I won the lottery. We lived conservatively, practiced delayed gratification and lived below our means while raising our six children.

When I turned 21, I set three goals: own a million-dollar business, own a million dollars in real estate and have a million dollars in the bank (with no debt to offset that bank balance). I wrote my goals down after I graduated from college. I've worked on them and have accomplished each goal individually, but have not been able to achieve them all at once.

My life has felt like the game "Sorry." You know the game, the one where you draw cards and move pieces around the board according to the card you draw. I had two pieces already around the board: a million-dollar business and a million in the bank. I was working my final piece around the board: a one-million-dollar home, no debt. Then the world of real estate went crazy; I'd just drawn the "Sorry – move back to the beginning" card.

It didn't stop there. By 2011, I was out of work and my $3 million real estate dream had turned into a $15,000/month sucking sound with personally guaranteed losses mounting. With no legitimate buyers in sight, it was clear I was headed toward multiple foreclosures.

Have you ever seen the light at the end of the tunnel and then come to the realization that it's a train heading at you? I was beside myself the morning I realized that my project was doomed. I didn't know what to do, so I began pacing the floor. After a few minutes of that, I decided to pace outside. I wasn't sure if I still had any options available or if all the decisions had already been made for me. Was there any way to mitigate the damage, or was I doomed to just watch this thing go down in flames?

Scream and Shout and Move On

My pacing turned into a self-loathing walk down the street and around the corner. I beat myself up verbally, trying to get the anger and regret out of my system. I remembered a time when I had gotten roughed up in a game as a teenage athlete. I was injured, and my coach told me to walk it off. This seemed like a good time to do exactly that. I went for a four-hour walk during which I told myself off. "You idiot! You fool! You've really screwed up this time. How could you do this to your family? You're supposed to be the protector. You should not have taken this risk. You should have known better. Your wife's going to leave you. Your children will hate you. You've lost all credibility. You're getting what you deserve. You're a pretender. You deserve to be poor."

After two hours of getting everything out of my head and literally yelling at myself out loud, a new thought hit me. *You can only beat yourself up for so long.* I asked myself, "Are you done yet?" My initial reaction was "No," so I went on ranting and raving at myself until finally I started to laugh and said, "Yes, I'm done now." I allowed myself to laugh at myself. How far was I going to walk? How long was I going to beat myself up? It occurred to me that I have just bought myself an education. It might have cost me a lot, but I had learned something for my million dollars.

After laughing at myself, I was able to clear my head and begin to think about what I was going to need to do to rebuild. I came to the realization that I had to walk back home and let my wife and six kids know I'd lost everything. I forced myself to face the truth: I was jobless, broke and facing multiple foreclosures. We were going to have to start over. But that was okay. I knew what I had to do, and while I wasn't thrilled about the idea, I knew the answer to the problem was work. I had worked myself into this situation and I was going to have to work my way out. But how?

I had once read that fear and faith are both beliefs. Fear is the belief that things will go poorly. Faith is the belief that things will go well. As I began my two-hour walk back home, I realized I needed to push out fear and act in faith. I needed to change my self-talk and the programming of my thoughts. Laughter is the best medicine, so I laughed.

New thoughts flooded my mind. I realized that I was the only person who could get me out of this mess. I also realized that I had made millions before, so I could do it again; how to do this was no longer a mystery. I knew I certainly wasn't going to do it in real estate because the real estate bubble had popped, but I knew I was capable of it.

The other thing I realized was I wasn't alone. A lot of people lost money in the real estate crash. I just happened to be one who timed it perfectly wrong. Right idea, wrong time. If the timing had been different, my plan would have worked. This helped me recognize that I was not a complete idiot. I simply had taken the risk at the wrong time.

One by one, the negative thoughts were pushed aside by positive thoughts. I remembered doing this on a smaller scale in the past. I reminded myself of this, saying, "Hey, you've done this before. This is exactly what you did when you were an inexperienced entrepreneur. Push fear aside and think positively. You know how powerful your thoughts can be."

By the time I got home, I was refocused on my three goals. I did not have a specific plan yet, but I felt confident that I would find a way. I also recognized that this hiccup in the plan allowed me a certain freedom; starting over meant we could do whatever we wanted. We were no longer tied to Dallas.

I will never forget explaining our situation to my wife.

"Well honey, I guess this means we can live wherever we want. Where would you like to live?"

"Wherever you are," she answered.

Those were the most precious words I'd ever heard. With those words, she affirmed that she was still my life partner, for better or worse. Not only was she committed to me, but also she knew exactly what to say to lift me up. Tears filled my eyes and flowed down my face.

Believe In Yourself, Bet On Yourself

The next day it was time to create a plan for rebuilding. Time to reinvent myself again. Small-time real estate developer was coming off my resume. What to do, what to do? I hadn't put together a resume in years. I left my last business to go into real estate development. As I searched the Internet for potential employers (and began competing with the mass of unemployed people flooding the job market), I experienced another jolt to my confidence. I wasn't sure where my skills would fit into the current job market. That shook me up. Who was I? How would I fit in?

I started helping friends and other people who were struggling in their businesses; this helped me to stop thinking about my own problems. I realized this helped me feel better, but beyond that, it also became my new mission in life. Over the years, I had learned a few things about building, scaling and selling businesses. As I shared my story, people asked me to help them with their business endeavors. I was afraid that sharing a failure would make people view me as a failure, but the opposite happened. People appreciated my honesty; by sharing about my experiences, I was able to earn trust and confidence.

To my relief, my problem was not a question of if I would get job offers (I got several); the problem was deciding if I wanted to work for someone else full-time or continue building my own consulting practice. Before long I had a dozen business owners as clients. I began putting them into small peer groups so they would benefit from each other's experiences, just like I was. Most business issues transcend business types. In other words, many businesses, even if they serve vastly different niches, share the same types of problems. The most common issues are challenges with people, inefficient business processes, ill-defined product-market fit, inability to take advantage of technology disruptions and ineffective use of digital marketing.

I decided to put my effort into building my own business, which was helping others with their businesses. I had come to realize that my identity — who I am — is not determined by my success or failure. I embraced my identity as an entrepreneur; I also embraced my role, which is to build businesses and inspire people. My target market is fellow entrepreneurs — risk takers trying to make their dreams come true that are willing to work hard, put in the time, money and effort required to make an idea a reality.

Through all this, I learned some very important lessons. I learned that the greatest asset is your brain; you have an incredible ability to solve problems, using your own wits. When you focus your brain on a problem and keep your goals in mind, the outcomes you encounter are not success or failure but rather new input to the problem-solving system. I also learned that even when you do everything right, sometimes external forces like the real estate bubble burst can take you out, so it's important to have a back-up plan.

After helping a handful of entrepreneurs scale and build their companies, I knew I could repeat these accomplishments again and again. I've done it for five years now. Working as a consultant helping other businessmen to become successful, is exceedingly rewarding both personally and financially. Interestingly enough, the lessons I learned from failure are the foundation of my success today. Because of this, I can confidently say that failure is an outcome, not a destination or destiny. When you hide your failures, you rob the world of the knowledge you've gained as you've worked through the obstacles to find success.

Failure is common. It's fundamental to the learning process. If you're facing a failure and the future looks bleak, you need to walk it off. If you're beating yourself up about something in your past, you need to scream and shout and move on. Invest in yourself and you will succeed. Have faith the answer is coming. I believe in you.

About the Author

Mike Tobias coaches entrepreneurs on selling and scaling their business ideas. Mike is a serial entrepreneur with over 30 years of building, growing and selling companies across diverse industries, including digital media, technology, telecommunications, financial services and manufacturing. He has raised over $80 million for his companies.

Mike is the Senior Partner at CGO Partners where he helps entrepreneurs fund, grow and sell their businesses. Mike's trusted reputation and experience as entrepreneur, operator and investor make him a valuable mentor in any transaction.

Mike can be reached at mike@cgopartners.com or follow his blog at www.cgopartners.com.

Chapter Nine

Growing Through Life's Lessons

By Louis Smith

"Adversity is God molding you for victories, as there is some benefit to be found in every adversity. The hurdles of life are not to trip you but to train you to jump higher."

~ Louis Smith

A military coup had recently failed in Umtata, the then capital of the republic of the Transkei. Dead bodies were strewn across the streets. Nausea was my constant companion, not only because of the putrid stench of decomposition, but also because of the evident apathy. So many lives had been lost. So little regard for life.

People lived in homes that resembled prisons, surrounded by tall security walls, electric fences, burglar alarms, guard dogs, steel security doors and barred windows. Friends were murdered in their beds while sleeping, others were executed in their living room in front of their families. This was not a distant threat from which I was isolated. The brutality hit close to home. Our farm manager, father to young children, had his tongue and male organs cut off before he was left to bleed to death. My parents were attacked repeatedly, most recently with people armed with AK47's, Russian-made machine guns. My grandpa never recovered from this attack; he lost the ability to speak.

One chilly evening as my wife, daughter and I were traveling home on a quiet farm road, we were startled by the sound of smashing glass, like a bomb detonating. A brick had smashed through our truck window, narrowly missing us and spewing fragments like shrapnel across the vehicle. With racing hearts, we checked on our precious daughter; to our relief, she was unharmed.

Exhausted after driving all day, we could finally see the beautiful shimmering ocean on the horizon. It was a perfect sunny African day, wildlife grazing green grass under thorn trees. We were on the way to spend family time with granny and grandpa at the beach. Whilst navigating a blind bend on a dusty, bumpy, unkempt road, we stumbled upon a terrifying scene. As far as I could see, chanting warriors swarmed like flies across the road and countryside, dressed, painted and ready for battle. Thinking this could be the end of our earth journey, I cried out, asking for divine intervention. I hit the brakes, skidding to a halt only inches from the ocean of warriors, engulfing us in a thick, choking, blinding dust. The warriors surrounded our car like a colony of bees, chanting, singing, stamping their feet and pounding on the hood, windows, and roof with their spears. The noise was deafening.

Seeing the terror in my wife's eyes, I shouted above the roar, "Don't make eye contact. Don't show fear. Look straight ahead," all the while praying for God's protection.

In that moment, I learned a life lesson that I have held to ever since: don't get distracted by your surroundings or circumstances. That information could terrify or discourage you. Instead, keep your eye on the goal.

I engaged the vehicle into four-wheel drive and crept forward, like a shoal of fish around a dolphin. The warriors moved out of the way, closing behind us as we edged forward. It seemed like an eternity passed as we slowly moved through the crowd, but eventually — praise God! —we were clear. We held hands in silence, tears in our eyes. Our speechlessness said it all. The truck was dented and beaten, but we'd survived, shaken yet unscathed.

Trained Terrorists

A platoon of well-trained terrorists, armed and equipped by Communist Russia to overthrow the Transkei, a small young country near the southern most point of Africa, attempted to land unnoticed at night in the isolated, impenetrable dense Dwesa jungle near our trading post. The terrorists had been spotted, so we were on high alert. The Dwesa nature reserve is an incredibly beautiful pristine piece of African coastal heaven, teaming with wildlife from small birds to enormous white rhino.

The battle raged for days; the rattle of machine gunfire filled the air. Bombs exploded round the clock, shaking the earth. Helicopters droned continuously, rallying troops and delivering food and supplies to the makeshift military base. Dust filled the sky, stirred up by the convoys of troop carriers, trucks, flame throwers and armored vehicles pouring in to take on the terrorists. The military blockaded roads; armed forces patrolled the streets and countryside. We lived under curfew; no one was allowed out of their homes between 6 p.m. and 6 a.m.

In the past, we had annually set up camp in this remote part of Africa, bringing in front-end loaders, dam scoops, trucks and many staff to stockpile sand and crushed shells, the raw materials used for the following year's brick manufacturing.

My incredible bride of three years, our three-month-old baby and I set up base in our family cottage, approximately a 60-minute drive from civilization (over atrocious roads). The cottage was rustic but beautiful, overlooking the beach. It was peaceful. Relaxing. Quiet and isolated. In a typical year, it was the perfect retreat and recovery destination. The home did not have electricity or any means of communication, nor were there neighbors, police or hospitals anywhere nearby. I left my darling bride there as I went to supervise the work, trusting that she would be safe despite the unsettling backdrop of the vibrations from the bomb blasts, machine gun fire, helicopters and the drone of surveillance planes that filled the air.

After another restless night (thanks to all the military activity) as I was leaving home that morning, my wife pleaded, "Darling, please get home before dark." We both knew that the military shoots first and asks questions later. Only days earlier, while driving close to home, my wife and I came across a military control point complete with military stop signs, enormous barricades and a small gap for vehicles to pass through. We stopped, but seeing no soldiers, we looked around and then at each other. Bewildered, we began to drive forward, still scanning the surroundings. Then I saw it – a machine gun barrel poking out of the tall grass. I slammed on the brakes, startling my wife. Soldiers armed to the teeth jumped out the grass, screaming at us as if we had done something wrong. After checking out our vehicle, they told us, "If you had driven off we would have shot you." They explained that they hid away as a precaution, in case we were terrorists.

We were shaken, to say the least.

Later that same day the news reported that another vehicle, at a similarly unmanned military roadblock, stopped and drove off. The occupants were mowed down, brutally executed in their vehicle.

Life is Unpredictable

On this particular day, the crimson African sun shimmered over the majestic Indian Ocean, set against clear blue sky and brightening the snow-white beaches. The tall green grass swayed gently in the warm breeze, completing the picture of African tranquility.

But in moments it went from tranquility to mayhem, testing my organizational skills, perseverance, determination and understanding.

While preparing to go home, the situation suddenly went from great to disastrous. Our fully loaded truck became stuck on the beach. This was a serious challenge because enormous waves were rapidly approaching due to the incoming tide. If we didn't get the truck moving soon, it would be pounded and submersed by the breakers.

Here I learned yet another lesson: to make informed decisions while remaining flexible. Any mistakes and we could have a second vehicle bogged down since the sand was incredibly soft; at this point, we were sinking down past our ankles. My efficient and faithful staff swung into action, hauling corrugated iron and long poles onto the beach. We placed them under the vehicle tires for grip and support. Then we strapped two trucks together, offloaded the cargo from the truck that was stuck. This took time, and at one point I thought we might lose the battle against the clock. The water was lapping the truck tires when the front-end loader heaved, lifting and pushing the back truck with its bucket as the front truck pulled. Joyful shouts filled the air as the vehicles came free onto solid soil.

We were still celebrating the victory when it occurred to me that time had flown away from us; it was too late to get the staff to their homes before the curfew. I had a critical decision to make: to value my safety or the safety of my staff. I believe servant leadership is the key to great team spirit and to the development of loyalty, trust and respect. I chose what I feel is the right choice: to lead by serving and protecting my people.

Finding accommodation for about fifty staff in this tense environment was a daunting challenge. Keep in mind, there were no hotels nearby. The military was vigilant about enforcing curfews. Time was ticking and lives were at stake, with only minutes to the 6 p.m. curfew. We knocked on the doors of local residents, negotiating, pleading and begging people to take my staff into their homes. By the time this was accomplished, the sun had sunk over the horizon, and it was past curfew. I was far from home and in deep trouble as the military had blockaded the roads.

The only way home was a near impassible dirt and grass track, which by daylight was treacherous. I drove this path at night, without lights of any kind. The path was steep and angled; rocks, boulders and ditches barred the way. I inched along in the dark, praying for God's guidance and protection so that the patrols would not spot me. Gripping the steering wheel and sweating from exhaustion and stress, nearly touching the windscreen to keep on the overgrown cattle track, I felt the ground give way beneath me. The truck slid sideways on slick black clay down a steep embankment into a tidal river, which was now too deep for the vehicle. Water rose over the hood as I tried to cross the river, and my truck sputtered and died as water flooded the engine. I had to climb out the window into the river, as the water level was too high for me to open the door. I prayed that my beautiful prized truck would still be there in the morning and not get washed downstream.

It was so dark I could hardly see my hands in front of me. In the still of the night, the fighting seemed closer and louder. Bomb blasts shook the earth, machine guns rattled relentlessly and massive flames from flamethrowers glowed in the distance, destroying the jungle as the military scourged out the terrorists.

Action Kills Excuses and Fear

I knew my wife would be worried, to say the least. We both knew the extent of the danger.

As I struggled to reign in the thoughts that swirled in my head, I reminded myself that I'd married a lady descended from generations of missionaries to Africa. I knew she would be reading the Word and praying, leaning on the incredible power of her Savior.

My heart pounded as I continued the seemingly endless journey home. It was only a 20-minute drive by day, but it was completely different in the pitch-black night. I lost the path frequently and tripped often. At times I stood deathly still, my heart thumping in my chest as I waited out mysterious noises that could have been either patrol members or terrorists.

When I finally arrived home hours later, I was sore, cut, bruised, bloodied, wet, exhausted, hungry and thirsty. I felt sorry for myself, but I was relieved to be out of the danger zone. All I wanted to do was to embrace my wife. However, instead of getting a nice warm welcome, my wife, who was beside herself with grief, screamed at me for having left her.

My first reaction was to be angry, but then I took a step back, tried to see the situation through her eyes and listened to her with all my heart. I reminded myself that she had only been back in South Africa for a short time, and the dangerous conditions were wearing on her. It's so easy to be self-centered, attacking and pointing fingers. I held her and listened to her until she calmed down, resisting the urge to defend myself. This is an important tactic for any relationship; only through listening to one another can we truly work together.

Learning the Important Lessons

Looking back on these challenges, I learned incredible lessons that can be applied to life and business experiences alike. It's important to have a well thought out strategic plan, but when disaster strikes, it is equally important to be flexible and to think on my feet. I discovered the power of action, since taking action kills fear. Even if the goal looks insurmountable, keep taking steps forward, one at a time, until you find success.

You have more inner strength and wisdom than you realize. Your God-given strengths are released in critical challenging times. It is tempting to wish away the challenges, but instead of asking God to remove obstacles, embrace the opportunity to grow to your full potential.

About the Author

Louis Smith was raised in rural South Africa, where his first language was Xhosa. He has dealt with adversity over and over, from dyslexia, to losing his home and farm due to political unrest and finally being stricken with leukemia.

Louis and his wife La-Verne are now living among the sequoias in California. They have four grown children and five grandchildren.

He is a Certified John Maxwell Coach, Certified Holistic and Nutritional Consultant, a motivational speaker and has shared the stage with Dr. Myles Monroe, Randy Gage and John Mason.

Contact him at
louisbaldeagle@gmail.com or WWW.LouisGsmith.com.

Chapter Ten

Who Said, "No Women Allowed?"

By April Krahl

"I can do all things through Christ Who Strengthens Me."

~ Philippians 4:13

Everyone thought I was crazy to dive headfirst into something that had never been done before in a male-dominated industry. Starting a business can be scary and even intimidating. Those close to me didn't understand why I wanted to do this; they seemed to think it was a bad idea or assumed I wouldn't do well being a woman majority owner, teaching an industry dominated by men. I did my best not to focus on their lack of support. In mid-2011 my husband and I started a company rooted in our experience in the insurance restoration industry. After traveling and working in different states we uncovered a tremendous need for the establishment of a standardized training program. This type of training simply did not exist in our industry.

At first I was unsure how this new concept would work in a practical sense. Being that it is a male-dominated industry, I was afraid I would not be taken seriously and would be judged and questioned on my knowledge. I knew there were plenty of owners with much more experience than I had. After all, we were teaching them how to run their businesses more efficiently and increase their sales.

I did my best to put those thoughts to rest and went to work. I was constantly marketing, marketing, marketing! Back then there was very little cash to float the new business, so I would cold call local companies on a daily basis. I experienced rejection after rejection. For this reason, I hated cold calling. Self-doubt crept in, and on many days I didn't have it in me to just pick up the phone and dial. I found myself making excuses to avoid the phone. I started wondering if this new company would go anywhere. Because we were still working out the kinks of the business, I was still getting comfortable with defining what our market needed and how to articulate our solution to potential customers.

I had to go above and beyond to prove my credibility. This kept me on my toes. I not only had to sell the training, but also I had to sell myself. They had to trust me first if they were going to buy. Through trial and error, I soon was able to show them something of value that customers could reliably use, and I gained respect in the industry. This helped grow my company's reputation. Whether this fact is acknowledged up front or not, I believe a man will always test a woman's knowledge when she tries to get into a male-dominated business or industry.

At first my self-doubt got in the way of my success. I worried that I wouldn't answer their questions to their satisfaction. Because I allowed these concerns to get to me, sometimes fear would overtake me and I felt stuck. However, I quickly recognized that I was my own biggest problem, and I started to use that fear as a motivator. I identified my fear of not having anyone at the training, and then I channeled that fear into action as I forced myself to pick up the phone and start dialing. Eventually, I became an expert at selling over the phone. It simply took practice and perseverance.

New battles sprung up each day. When it came to booking meeting spaces, every hotel wanted guaranteed room nights. We didn't have the money for hotel rooms; we just needed a meeting space. Surely, there are local companies who needed event spaces and without rooms, right? How could they not understand this? Some days I just hung up the phone and screamed. After many calls, I finally found a hotel that would work with us. They took a chance on our new company, beginning a great relation-ship that benefited both parties. That was a relief.

Once we had the meeting space arranged, I marketed like crazy. However, even with all the work I had poured into my marketing efforts, we only sold the first training session to seven men. After the first break, two of the seven walked out and never came back. I was scared this might cause a chain reaction; I was terrified that the rest of the men in attendance would also walk out. Instead of telling my business partner that they left because they thought it was terrible, I told him that they had to leave for a company emergency and hoped to be back next day. I did this so he would not get demoralized or lose focus on the five men we still had in attendance. That was tough, but by the end of the first training, the five that stayed were glad they did. As we moved forward, we learned more and more about how to make the training sessions more informative and helpful, and each consequent training session got bigger and better. Together, we were a team.

It was an exciting time, but it was far from easy. Every day was a hustle. We hosted a training session once every 6-8 weeks. Then, surprise! I found out I was pregnant. This was a pleasant surprise, but we were both simultaneously very excited and scared. The business was still in its infancy, and we were living training session to training session. We knew a new baby would require a lot of money and time, and we just didn't know what to expect.

Some of our family members discouraged us from continuing our new business. They told us to find stable and reliable work since we had a baby on the way. There were days when I cried and wanted to give up but I just decided to work harder. Instead of letting anxiety get the best of me, I poured my energy into marketing and refining my processes. I had invested a lot into this business, and I had faith that it was a viable business that would succeed if I just kept at it.

After multiple training sessions, I realized that the repetitive nature of the business was exhausting me. The business needed to be scaled. An idea came to me: what if we held an event that featured several speakers? I talked to clients daily and they told me exactly what they wanted to learn. I told my business partner the subjects our clients were interested in learning about, and we started to design an event that would meet their needs.

Time was short; I wanted to organize the event before my son arrived. At this point, we had six speakers and five corporate sponsors, so we had to deliver. I was excited and nervous, especially since my partner had promised the sponsors that the event would be 70 percent bigger than our largest training to date. I was shocked and intimidated. How was I supposed to deliver such results?

At times I felt like I was carrying the world on my shoulders. It was just too much stress, since the responsibility to fill the events fell completely on me. I felt overwhelmed and in desperate need of help. I was mad at my partner because he refused to pick up the phone and recruit attendees. Our online sales were minimal, and it was necessary to talk one-on-one with attendees at that time. I also was tasked with learning how to use new software that was integral to our business. It was a lot of pressure for just one person, especially since I was about to be a new mom.

Just over a week before I was due, the doctor informed me that my son was breech. I had to decide whether I wanted to try to give birth naturally or via C-Section. I decided on the C-Section. When I checked into the hospital, I only had 13 people registered for the first Summit, which was less than a month away. I did my best to remain calm, but I was on edge. All I wanted to do was focus on becoming a new mom, but this was not possible.

My son was born, and when I heard that first cry it was the most amazing sound I had ever heard. Life had just begun and I was so happy. However, much as I felt deep love for my baby, I felt distant from my husband. He cried when our son was born and was very happy to meet him, but I felt I had no support from him whatsoever. My mom flew in on the day I was cleared to go home from the hospital, and I was very happy that she was there to help with the baby. She stayed for 11 days, and while I was grateful for her help, I was also shocked by how little my husband interacted with our newborn son. He would only hold him for a couple minutes each day. I cried when she went home because I knew that I was completely on my own.

My recovery was very slow and I experienced a lot of pain from the procedure; getting around was really tough. I had to do something that I told myself I would never do. I had to sell out the event, so I put our newborn son into daycare only 12 days after he was born. This was horrible for me; I wanted him right by my side. I didn't need this extra stress as a new mom; plus, I was supposed to be resting so I could recover. I was not sleeping at all; the baby was not breast-feeding and I had to constantly pump. To my dismay, my husband never helped at night, not even once. I was completely exhausted each day, operating on two to maybe three hours of sleep.

This wreaked havoc on me. All I wanted to do was quit, enjoy being a new mom and get some sleep. Why was it my sole responsibility to make this event a success? Why couldn't he step up and let me take care of our son? I kept asking myself if it was even worth it. To get through this difficult time, I repeatedly recited Philippians 4:13 to myself: "I can do all things through Christ who strengthens me." I prayed constantly for the strength to get through each day. I felt as though getting through this event with a new baby was my Mount Everest. Yet I had a strong desire and determination to succeed, so I kept on climbing.

At that time, our company's reputation was on the line. We had corporate sponsors and had promised a sold out event; it was do or die. I had no choice but to make it a success if we wanted to continue this business. Each day I worked myself to exhaustion, even through sleep deprivation.

I did it! After what felt like the longest weeks of my life, the final outcome was a sold-out event. I even sold over the initial goal! What a relief. It was the toughest thing I'd ever had to do.

I look back at that time and marvel that I survived. I wanted to give up so much, but I'm glad I didn't because that successful event propelled us into a nationwide brand in the industry. We gained numerous corporate sponsors and attendees from all over the United States.

From this experience, I've learned that success is right around the corner — even if you are just about to give up. I also learned that the Lord is with me and He gives me the strength I need to go forward.

Over the last few years there have been many times that I've wanted to quit. I can plan an event months out and expect hundreds of people and the majority typically won't register until three to four weeks out. I rely on past successes to help me hit my goals, and I find the successes build upon themselves. I enjoy the results because our attendees always leave with information that changes their business and lives for the better. It feels good to help others succeed.

Here's what I want you to take away from my experiences: no matter how many times you've experienced success, doubt and fear can sink in. Don't let it.

Refer back to your past successes to propel you into future successes. Find someone who can mirror what you do so you don't have to rely solely on yourself; this will relieve a lot of stress. Most importantly, listen to your heart's desire. Maybe you are starting a new business and everyone around you is telling you not to do it. Ask yourself if you would regret not doing it. If so, then go for it! I believe it's true that a person will always regret the things they chose not to do, over the easy things that they chose to do.

So, when you are tired, keep at it. Don't quit, because your success is right around the corner!

About the Author

April Krahl was born in Paradise, California. She has lived in many states and now calls Texas her home. If she could live anywhere she prefers to have the ocean in her back yard. April enjoys spending time with her son, family and friends. She is the majority owner of Elite Consulting Pro, IRC Summit, the sole owner of Storm Consultants, LLC and is a Certified Brian Tracy Sales Trainer. April is a self-motivated professional in business consulting, market strategy, advertising, promotion, product pricing, and sales. She's an expert in marketing concepts from inception to execution and launching new products and events, and is a seasoned sales trainer, focused on achieving continuous, improved business success.

She can be reached at Aprilkrahl@gmail.com.

Chapter Eleven

Never Give Up: How I Rescued My Family From A Life Of Pain

By Angeline Wehmeyer

"Winners never quit and quitters never win."

~ Vince Lombardi

My dream ever since I was a young girl was to come to the land of opportunity and build a wonderful family and career. I spent many lonely nights away from my family as they worked far away on the border of China and Vietnam. My mother and father sacrificed their personal lives and health and worked long hours to provide for our family. They stayed in a dingy apartment that was a 24-hour car ride away from me. They spent most days in the hot sun processing shipments between the two countries. The only breaks they got were to sleep, and then they were at it again. The conditions at the border were terrible. The air was filled with smog from the idling trucks, and the dirt roads left a layer of dust and filth on everything.

Growing up, I only got to see my parents once or twice a year. Most of the time, I felt like a foster kid. I stayed with various aunts and uncles, depending on the circumstances. I vividly remember crying in the shower and wishing my life could be different. I wondered, "Why do other kids' parents always show up in the teacher/parent meetings, but not mine?" My parents did not even attend the significant events that happened in my life. They were always too busy and too far away.

When I graduated from high school and left for college, I was so excited. When I stepped on campus for the first time, I was filled with pride and enthusiasm to take my life to the next level. As I hauled my possessions into my dorm room, I looked over and saw my roommates unpacking many boxes of new stuff with their parents by their side. The feelings of loneliness and longing swept over me, obscuring the thrill of starting college. It took me a while, but I stopped myself from wallowing in self-pity. I reminded myself of my dream and how close I was to accomplishing it. My childhood was very difficult, but I choose to believe that those hard times strengthened and prepared me for the road ahead. This attitude helped me succeed, even without the parental support most of my peers enjoyed.

My final bittersweet moment was when I graduated from college. I was a straight-A student, and I was the only person selected to give the commencement speech to the entire school. It was one of the proudest moments of my life. However, when I looked out at the audience and realized that my parents hadn't made it to witness this important milestone, I felt the pain of their absence. At the same time, I understood that they would have come if they could have. Feeling lonely when surrounded by hundreds of people is a unique type of sadness. It took everything in me to suppress that feeling and stand proudly in front of all those people.

After graduating college in China, I set my sights on my main goal: to go to the United States. My unwavering goal was to fulfill my childhood dream to be a successful businesswoman so I could provide for my family. I had been away from my parents since I was eight years old, so I'd always been a self-starter and very independent. I applied to a university in the United States called Farleigh Dickinson. One of my unwavering convictions was that I needed to study and work hard so in the future I could provide for a good life for my parents. They had sacrificed so much to support me, I desperately wanted to one day return the favor.

When I arrived in the United States, I was determined to keep the momentum going. To that purpose, I enrolled in a master's course in entrepreneurial studies. I gave everything I had, even though I faced many challenges. English is my second language, so some of the coursework proved very tedious and/or confusing.

I graduated from Farleigh Dickinson after two years, having obtained my master's degree. I was on top of the world! I was ready to enter the workforce and start earning some real money. I thought this was the best path forward to reach my goals, but I had no idea how wrong I was. In actuality, I was about to learn another important life lesson.

I joined a fashion company that sold custom sandals for women. I really wanted to help them reach their maximum potential and make a difference. I worked long hours and always tried to improve everything I touched. I was looking for recognition, but the company couldn't have cared less. When I approached my boss about taking on more responsibility, they gladly gave it to me, but they did not provide a pay increase or even promise of a better title or position in the company. I realized that I was just a cog in the machine of the company. In their eyes, I was a dispensable commodity with a set value. I realized that, at this pace, it would take a lifetime to reach my goals.

I was very discouraged by this experience, so I decided to shift my focus to my first goal, which was to start a family. I needed something to ground me; I was searching for tangible rewards. I had come so far that I refused to look back or give up.

I got married and had two wonderful children. I took time off work and devoted myself to my family, finding fulfillment in that role. Still, something nagged at me, alerting me that something was off. Everything was going great, but something was missing. I still wasn't fulfilling my childhood dream. I needed to get back on track.

I considered my options. I knew I couldn't become an employee again; it just wasn't for me. I needed something of my own where I could see the fruits of my labor. I had my first breakthrough after reading the book "Rich Dad, Poor Dad." The book taught me that to become wealthy you needed to work smart, not hard. I also learned that I needed to be a business owner, not an employee. This way I could make my money work for me instead of trading time for money. I could also have time freedom and the ability to experience all that the world has to offer.

After much deliberation, I decided to start an online business selling children's accessories. I made some connections in China and brought in some cute stuff that I thought women would love. Unfortunately, I quickly found out that just having a good idea wasn't enough to be successful in business. After investing over $10,000 of my husband's hard-earned money, the business failed. We were stuck with the inventory we ordered with no means to sell it.

After that loss, I felt discouraged again. I felt guilty and ashamed. I didn't want to feel like that forever, so I started taking various investment courses and attending networking seminars. Around this time, I was actively investing in real estate. This looked like a new avenue for me, something I could get behind. But that too, fell apart. One day I got a call from my realtor and everything came crashing down. One of the houses I had bought had over $40,000 in foundation issues, and I had to come up with the cash to fix it. That same feeling of discouragement and shame rushed over me, but this time it was so much worse. I cried my eyes out when I told my husband what had happened. It seemed like I was destined to fail. I was so fearful that I just didn't have what it takes to be a successful businesswoman. I was strongly considering just throwing in the towel and getting a regular job like before.

This is the point in my story where I realized that it's okay to rest, but it's important that you never quit. I knew that I needed to find some way to make money while mitigating the risk. We didn't have any more money to lose. I attended more networking and business events, seeking out the right opportunity.

This took some time and effort, which was hard to do considering the experiences I'd had. But even after all of those hardships, I wasn't willing to throw in the towel. I couldn't let my parents down, not after all they had done for me. While attending one of these events, the opportunity found me. I was approached by a woman in the health and wellness industry, and she opened my eyes to a world of opportunity and a healthier lifestyle for me and my family. She said, "Angeline, what good is wealth if you don't have good health?" That struck a nerve with me because I thought of my parents, working so hard in the hot sun and trading their health for my freedom. I needed to give back to them. And why stop there when I could also help others do the same?

As always, my philosophy was if you want something, you need to work hard for it. I quickly realized that my online business didn't work out because number one, it wasn't my passion, and number two, I didn't feel fulfillment from the pursuit of it.

Growing my business wasn't easy. I was raising two children and I had to battle the seeds of doubt from my previous failures. I kept pushing forward, keeping my childhood vision in mind. This was the rock that guided to me to success. I truly believe that you are destined to fail if you do not have a strong purpose and vision. Like my previous businesses, I faced many challenges. Of particular difficulty was the rejection I faced from my own friends and family. When I approached them about my business, they were very negative and tried to convince me to go back into the workplace. They treated me as if I wasn't capable. It hurt very much to have the people I loved exhibit a lack of faith in me. I already was struggling with a lot of uncertainty. But instead of giving up, I decided to block that out and press on.

Once I started building my team, I felt like things were moving in the right direction. Then the reality of how difficult this really was set in again because I started losing team members at a rapid pace. They were quitting because they couldn't handle the rejection and the hard work required to be successful. It was so disappointing to see them abandon their dreams so easily. Some of them gave up right away because of the same type of pressure I had received from my friends and family. I couldn't believe they would let someone else steal their dream. I watched these people suffer, but there was nothing I could do about it. I could not make decisions for them, but I could choose to persevere with my own goals. I decided I would never give up. I stopped being angry and realized that I couldn't force someone to be successful. They have to truly want it for themselves.

I invested heavily in learning the necessary mindset and skills required to build and grow a business. Through this, I realized many people have uphill dreams but have downhill habits. What I mean by this is they are willing to settle for less, they let fear get in their way and they surrender to fear. I learned that you need to foster a burning desire if you wish to succeed. My burning desire was to create a lifestyle filled with freedom for my family and ultimately support for my parents. This desire fuels the willpower to push through the tough times and keep moving, even when it looks like there is no hope.

After you have a clear picture of what you want, you need to make a commitment that you are going to make it happen no matter what. You have to envision yourself already accomplishing your goals and convince yourself that you can get there.

Today, I focus on my daily activities. I make every day a masterpiece. I commit to the belief that the only day that counts is today. There's no time to major in minors or waste time on tasks that don't have any significance. I focus on doing the right thing, and I detach myself from the outcome so that I can remain on track through good times and bad. As long as I focus on the right things and stay consistent, the outcome eventually comes.

Having your own business isn't easy. You have to take the hits and keep moving forward. Never let average people bring you down with their average mindset. Don't let them steal your dreams. Hold on to them, cherish them and fight like hell to make them a reality. Be outstanding, be exceptional, and when you least expect it, you will reach your destination.

About the Author

Angeline Wehmeyer has always been an entrepreneur at heart. Since a young age she learned to fend for herself. After achieving her Master's Degree in entrepreneurial business, she went on to start many successful companies. She is fluent in three languages and has invested heavily in personal improvement courses to sharpen her skills. Through her many businesses Angeline has created multiple streams of income. She has extensive knowledge of building companies from the ground up. Her passion is to share her system with others in order to constantly add more value and help them create a lifestyle filled with joy.

Website: www.angelinewehmeyer.com

Chapter Twelve

Superheroes May Rest, But They Don't Ever Quit

By Ron Jones

"You're going to make a difference. A lot of times it won't be huge, it won't be visible even. But it will matter just the same."

~ Commissioner James Gordon

Don't Ever Quit, Even if it Hurts!

As I rocked my 14-month-old grandson and sang "You Are My Sunshine," tears rolled down my cheeks. The sweetness of the moment transported me to a time I now regretted. A time when I made choices that took me away from my son. You see, I wasn't there when my son needed me to hold him. Comfort him. Rock him to sleep.

Not only did I miss these crucial moments with my son, but also with my daughters. My daughters who have grown up and become beautiful, caring, intelligent, loving women.

Now that time has passed and I have gained perspective, I ask myself: Why? Why was I so self-centered and selfish? How did I miss the obvious — the fact that these were fleeting, precious opportunities?

I looked at my grandson as he slept peacefully, and I thanked God for giving me another chance. A chance to redeem myself, to become the superhero that I was born to be.

My whole worldview shifted six years ago, during an otherwise mundane and ordinary experience. I was at Costco, performing a routine and otherwise unimportant shopping trip, when I received the phone call that would shatter my world in ways I didn't imagine possible.

"Your son died," said the voice on the other end of the line.

It took me a few seconds to comprehend the message my father had just delivered. My world shrank and my senses went numb. "What happened?" I asked, barely being able to speak the words.

"He committed suicide."

Everything came to a screeching halt. I couldn't move, couldn't speak, couldn't even remember why I was there or what I was supposed to do. It was as if someone had sucker punched me in the stomach. I couldn't breathe. I couldn't cry. I couldn't form a rational thought.

I just kept asking, "Why? Why did this happen?"

Memories swirled in my head. Questions and thoughts mixed and collided. The weight of the world crashed down upon me.

Reality set in. This was a problem I could not fix. I would never see my son again. I could not bring him back. He was gone.

Tears streamed down my face. I stood there in the middle of Costco, unaware of passersby, unable to think anything but how much I wanted my son back. How desperately I wanted to turn back time, reverse the clock and make different decisions. I wanted to hold him. I needed to tell him I loved him. And now it was too late.

I was so angry with myself. I was angry with other people and at the circumstances and pressures that had influenced me to make choices that I now wished I could reverse. Those choices had taken me away from my son, now gone forever.

Pushing Past Anger and Regret

For a time, I was paralyzed. I was grieving, naturally, as only any parent who has lost a child can understand.

Eventually, I realized that my anger wasn't productive. I could not get my son back, but I could move forward. I needed to move through my grief and regret and use my newfound perspective to honor my son. I would change the way I lived my life so that I could positively impact others.

I had already learned a lot about the power of the mind. The things we think about define us. As such, our thoughts have the power to make or break us.

I also thought about how much I used to love superheroes as a young boy, and now, as an adult, I began to accept the fact that it was too late be a superhero to my son.

When I first got the news about my son, I blamed circumstances and other people for the choices I had made. Later, as I came to terms with the finality of the situation, I realized there was no one to blame. The fact was that the events that had happened were already done, and there was no way I could go back to change any of it.

However, I did have the power to choose how I moved forward. I could choose the way I would let this situation impact me. I could use it to create change for myself, my family, my business, my communities and eventually you, the reader. This is how I can honor the memory of my son. I have learned that no matter what happens in our lives, we have the power to choose how we respond. We have free agency to make choices that will positively impact those around us. We can become superheroes.

What is a Superhero?

Each one of us is endowed with an extraordinary gift — the potential to become a real-life superhero. Within each person lies a dormant power that is waiting to be activated.

Being a superhero does not mean you have to be able to lift up a car and fly, or weave a web, or even have specialized gadgets to help you save the city from thugs. It only requires that you take the actions necessary to live your life from an empowered place.

Superheroes don't allow their environment, circumstances or the people around them to dictate how they show up in life. Instead, they are masters at responding and influencing without succumbing to the influence of negative people or situations.

They are also people who care about the wellbeing of others. They are people who take it upon themselves to become leaders, mentors, good parents, inspiring teachers, counselors, great listeners and nurturing grandparents.

My First Superhero!

When I was a little kid, I was fascinated by superheroes. They could do things I only dreamed of. They appeared to be beyond human, and I sure wanted to be as extraordinary as they were.

For the most part, I would be willing to wager most of us view ourselves as being very far removed from the ideal. What I didn't clearly see, however, was that behind the suit lived a man or woman who had to deal with problems just like everybody else.

I remember vividly having to shine shoes in order to make a buck if I wanted to purchase the extras that were not included in my mom's single-parent budget. I never felt shame in doing work to earn extra money, but I also didn't know that someone who was not even related to me might one day want to provide for me.

My first superhero was my stepdad. He came into my life when I was only nine years old. One day I wanted to go to the movies with some friends, so I proceeded to take my step stool, shining rag and shoe polish and set up shop so I could earn the necessary money. When my step-dad saw me leaving, he asked me what I was doing.

The thing that happened next changed my life forever. He looked me in the eye and said, "Ronnie, I'm here for you now. You don't need to go shine shoes to make money anymore. Here's some money; go have fun with your friends."

It was a gesture both simple and yet profound in its impact, because up until that point, I didn't think anyone loved me enough to do such a thing for me. I knew my mother loved me, but I understood she couldn't afford to give me extra things. What changed me wasn't so much that I didn't have to shine shoes anymore, but the realization that someone cared deeply about me and was willing to take care of me. That made me realize that superheroes are those who make a difference in another person's life.

A Superhero in the Making

How many times have you witnessed a child pretending to be his or her favorite superhero character? They ask to have a sheet or towel wrapped around their necks; they stretch their arms out and pretend to fly. Sometimes they punch and kick as if fighting the bad guy and fall down as if being attacked, and in the end, they are always victorious in their battles.

As adults, many of us experience something similar; however, the battle is usually not "out there" but within. We try to dominate others by pressuring them into buying our stories and ideas; we kick and punch when people don't act the way we want them to; we allow ourselves to be knocked down by the limitations that we either impose on ourselves or were imposed on us by things out of our control, like an illness or a company layoff. And yet, there is still a part deep within us that desires to thrive, to be victorious, and to overcome. That desire to thrive is the birthplace of the superhero.

In my own life, there have been many instances in which I allowed my insecurities, fears and circumstances to influence my behavior. I became a millionaire at the age of 30, but then I lost it all — my marriage, my family, my house, my business, my financial security and nearly my health. Why did this happen? Because I had become complacent in my relationships and in my business affairs; I wrongly assumed I was untouchable. I had become somewhat arrogant and allowed external influences to define me. As a result, I made decisions that resulted in tremendous loss.

It wasn't until I was stripped of my earthly possessions that I realized that my potential lay in my ability to influence my environment by, first and foremost, taking charge of my emotions. I could first become the superhero in my own life, saving myself, and then I could go on to become a superhero dad, boss, friend and so on.

I'm so grateful that I have the opportunity to be a mentor, or, as I like to say, a super pawpaw to my grandchildren. As I am reminded of the path I took to get to where I am today — losing my marriage, possessions, son and the opportunity to mentor my daughters while they were growing up, I can't help but think that it's funny how the universe works sometimes.

I had to go through those experiences for me to wake up and make better choices in how I treat both others and myself. I am now embracing the opportunity to be a superhero to my grandchildren and others around me. I have discovered that my most potent superpowers are brought forth by my relationship with these wonderful people. Watching them grow into young ladies and gentlemen (never losing their superpowers — at least not in my eyes) is what empowers me to grow and share my experience, knowledge and wisdom with them and with you, the reader.

Activate Your Inner Superhero

Becoming a superhero spouse, parent, grandparent, family member, friend, leader, manager, teacher, coach, speaker, employee or just a better human being, means that you must think, be, and act like a superhero! Superheroes understand that circumstances do not dictate life choices. When things happen to superheroes, they don't get caught up in emotion; instead, they take action dictated by rational thoughts. Superheroes think rationally and act proactively, instead of reacting to events. You may find fame and fortune, but if you don't maintain rational and sober estimation of your options (refusing to react emotionally), you will not activate the superhero within.

Becoming a superhero takes work. It requires commitment. Action. Logical planning and foresight. Most importantly, it requires perseverance. You may get tired, and you may need to rest and gain perspective, but you must not quit.

I know far too well the consequences of reacting to emotions. I have lived it all. I have been poor and ordinary; I have been wealthy and extraordinary. I have experienced poverty and riches, both in my financial and personal life. Over the course of my life journey, I have learned that helping others is the most rewarding of all.

I hope this simple chapter touches you. Never quit your dreams, the dreams that empower you to create a super world for yourself, your family and the planet.

About the Author

Ron Jones started in the real estate business launching and growing a real estate investment company, residential and commercial real estate business, mortgage company and construction company to become a millionaire before the age of twenty-seven.

After losing everything before the age of 30, Ron went to college studying psychology and became a counselor for nine years, followed by various jobs before pursuing a career in the insurance industry.

If you asked Ron what his true passion is, he would tell you that it is his wife, two daughters, three stepdaughters, five son's-in-love, nine grandsons and three granddaughters.

www.superheroeslife.com
rjones08@att.net
817-734-7400

Chapter Thirteen

Expect The Unexpected

By François Sylvain

"Spirit never expresses itself other than perfectly. The imperfections are in our individual or collective ways of thinking."

~ Bob Proctor

As long as I can remember, I have been driven to add value. Whenever I am able to help an individual or to make the world a better place, I seize the opportunity. My commitment to making a difference has led me to struggles and victories, but it has never let me down. As I have traveled around the world, I've learned to trust in this one principle: if you allow yourself to care deeply, you can move mountains.

I first reaped the benefits of this principle when I helped my brother, an artist who was struggling to promote his art. I recognized his talent as a painter, but I also saw that he lacked marketing and people skills. I am a people person. I love to talk to strangers, and I find it easy to make connections.

I felt called to do something to help my brother, so I promoted his work in Europe and in the United States for the following four years. Our efforts were successful; in the USA alone, I established a network of over 250 distributors and retail outlets in over 25 states.

This experience benefited more than just my brother. I also benefited from the experience, because I learned something very important as I traveled around the world and met with a wide range of people. I met interesting people; I made friends. I embraced the diversity of accents, customs and cultures that I found in the many regions I visited. Most importantly, I came to understand that we are one big family. Every single person on this planet is part of the larger familial unit. We all have value; we all have something to contribute.

This revolutionized my worldview.

In 1979, the United States experienced a severe recession, bringing the business to a standstill. My customer base was the upper middle class, and the discretionary income necessary to buy art shriveled up.

We were living in California and my wife had just given birth to my oldest daughter; I now had four mouths to feed. Sales dwindled and money ran short, so I made the difficult decision to pause my career as an art agent and to take a sales position in Canada, intending to resume when the recession was over. Sadly, my brother passed away prematurely. I took solace in the fact that I had been able to help him experience success as an artist for several years. I helped him leave his legacy.

As a sales representative, I sold mostly through distributors. I was exceptionally successful at getting my distributors' employees to promote my products and won multiple sales contests and awards. Soon I was promoted to a supervisory position, heading up one of the company's three divisions.

At first, everyone at the head office was welcoming. However, two years into the job, the heads of the other two divisions began to openly attempt to sabotage my division. Why did they do this? I can only assume that they found my success threatening, since my division was doing exceedingly well.

They devised a plan to slow the growth of my division. Things started to mysteriously go awry. Orders for my products would get lost or partially shipped or the wrong products shipped. Naturally, this affected my sales record. Our clients started to complain and were told that the problem was my "poor communication skills."

My efforts to restore a climate of teamwork did not change their attitude. Eventually, the CEO asked for my resignation. Naturally, I moved on.

I was devastated at first, but I would soon find out that good can emerge from painful experiences. Soon the universe would place me in a situation where I would play an even more important role.

At this time, the real estate market was hot. I was quite handy in regards to home renovation, having learned many skills from my father, so I decided that I would find a house that had potential and fix it up. In my previous position, I had traveled a great deal and often been away from my family. This new pursuit would enable me to spend valuable time with my wife and children.

I had already renovated the house we were living in, so I first put it up for sale. It sold in one day. I then found a four-story Queen Anne revival-style house in a nearby town that met my criteria. It needed a lot of loving care, but it was positioned on a street of very nice homes and the neighborhood was definitely upscale.

I jumped on this opportunity. I would fix up the house; this would benefit both us and our new neighbors, since their property values would increase and I would make a profit. When my neighbors learned of my intentions, they were extremely pleased and friendly.

It took me 18 months to complete the work. The house looked great and the town designated it a Heritage Home.

Shortly after we listed our property with a real estate agent, we received an offer. The catch was: the offer was conditional upon the town council's approval of a change of zoning because the property was slated for use as a shelter for battered women.

When my neighbors learned about the prospective use of the home, they got very upset. The *not in my backyard syndrome* divided the town for a year. Every week, people wrote in the local newspaper to voice their opposition to or acceptance of the project. I also contributed articles, trying to promote amicable discussion and awareness of the humanitarian side of the shelter. Unfortunately, one of the loudest protesters was our neighbor, who made his feelings known to us.

Despite my best efforts, the prominent people living on my street won the battle and the shelter was established in another town. Shortly after that, we sold our house and moved away.

After that, I *rested* for a while. I took a break from caring so much about others and focused on my family and myself. However, I did not let this discouraging experience squelch my determination to help others. I did not stop caring; I simply took a short rest so that I could rise up and again pursue worthy causes once I had regained my strength.

Years later, I was in Costa Rica, living my dream of residing in a tropical climate when I once again heeded the call to make a difference.

While in Costa Rica, I met a Canadian couple that shared an amazing story of determination. They had been separated from their young daughter by a set of circumstances. For three years, they fought to be reunited with their daughter. Obstacles arose, and they spent thousands of dollars, but even when they exhausted all the options available to them in their home country, they continued to fight. At long last they won, against overwhelming odds.

The embers had been burning low, but this story rekindled my desire to care about others and create a better world. I decided to share their story in a book titled *Come Home, Sweetie*.

During my time in Costa Rica, I also saw how many foreigners were desperate to leave the country. Some lost their life savings and others, their lives. They had been seduced by the rosy picture of Costa Rica painted by the different entities promoting the country.

This distressed me, so I sought ways to help. Through my interactions with native Costa Ricans, I did my best to correct the distorted view that many have of foreigners. I also resolved to help would-be visitors, investors and residents by sharing my knowledge of the country with the foreigners I met. As part of my effort to promote harmony, I wrote a book titled *The Costa Rica No One Talks About*. It is my desire that my book will be a catalyst that brings a change of mindset and true sustainable development for Costa Rica and that we will join forces to create a climate of appreciation and gratitude for each other's unique qualities and contributions.

It is said that we are the sum of our experiences. These experiences detailed here jump-started my spiritual quest for answers. Why, as a species, do we choose pain over happiness, war over peace, and hatred over love? Why can't humans accept and appreciate their differences and live in harmony? What can I do to help us all get along?

I meditated and read a lot. Then I landed on an English website produced by a church organization. Their articles answered some of my questions. Their message of tolerance and collaboration and their vision of universal embracing of good values resonated with my desire to bring people together to work in harmony.

The church had a multi-lingual site, so I went on their French website intending to forward an article to a friend who did not know English. The translation was horrible, and I realized I could be of service. I communicated with the church's editor-in-chief and ended up translating several articles for him. After he had my translations assessed, he asked me if I wanted to be the coordinator of the French translations of the church materials. I accepted the position.

I put a team together and in less than two years the French website ranked second for number of visitors, just behind English. Needless to say, the church's administrators and members were extremely pleased with the results.

Since I also knew Spanish, I was asked to manage translations for the Spanish website as well. I put together a team of translators, and in less than a year, the Spanish website ranked fourth for site traffic.

At the time, the church did not have an Italian membership or website. The church's editor-in-chief learned that an Italian who had produced a website promoting similar values was using excerpts from the church's articles on his website.

The church's editor-in-chief asked me to communicate with the Italian and threaten him with court action if he didn't stop. I refused on the grounds that the Italian was adding his voice to ours to create a better world and therefore shouldn't be stopped. Many church members agreed with me. However, the church's editor-in-chief would not budge. I resigned, and two-thirds of the members left the church.

Was that a failure? Not at all. Those who left stood up for their values. They chose peace over war and tolerance and goodwill over small-mindedness. Many smaller groups sprung up; since then, many of these small groups have contributed to the promotion of those values.

Shortly after that, I learned of the term "personal development" and the law of attraction. I then realized I had been involved in the field of personal development without even knowing about the industry. As I learned more about personal development, I became aware that I was able to make a positive impact because of my devotion to caring deeply and my driving desire to bring people together in harmony. In fact, my commitment to caring and pursuing positive change had influenced people in every one of these situations.

With this perspective in mind, I reviewed my efforts. The shelter was built in another town, but was that a failure? Not at all; it was a great victory! On a personal level, I achieved my goal of increasing my neighbors' property value and I turned a profit. On a societal level, this incident raised awareness of the plight of victims of marital violence. As I reviewed the opinions published in the paper (of those in favor of the project), I was impressed by their compassion and desire to help those in need.

My children also learned many lessons, one of which is that decisions must be rooted in personal conviction, and they must not allow themselves to be swayed by what others think or say. It also taught them to consider other opinions with respect and to stand up for their beliefs. This experience built character.

I wanted to improve the world around me, and I have achieved that objective. I have demonstrated that when we work together towards a common goal, we can achieve great things and enjoy tremendous success. I have helped raise the level of awareness of thousands to the importance of caring for each other and edifying each other as we each contribute, using our unique skills and talents to better the world.

We all have something to contribute; each and every one of us can, in so many ways, work together to create a world where we can all flourish and live in peace and harmony.

When I acted upon my commitment to care deeply and help others, the spirit produced exceptional and greater results than I had imagined possible.

It is my desire that my experiences inspire you to act boldly on your heart's desires. Share your talents with the world. When you contribute to the global pool of positivity, we all benefit.

About the Author

François Sylvain is an entrepreneur, author, coach and investor. He also works as an independent consultant. He is active in the personal development industry and wrote *The Creative Powers Of Our Thoughts*, a self-help book that talks about how our thoughts create our future.

Raised in Montreal, Canada, he began his working life traveling extensively throughout Europe and the USA promoting the art of his brother, who was a painter. After an exceptionally successful career in sales and marketing, François went to Costa Rica to live his dream of residing in a tropical climate.

François uses his passion for travel to learn about other cultures and bring people together, irrespective of nationality, language, faith or convictions, to help create a world where mankind may live in peace and harmony. He is a father of four and grandfather of six.

Find him at FrancoisSylvain.com and HealthAndWealthAttraction.com

Chapter Fourteen

Seeing The Sun Beyond The Mountains

By Marie Rosy Toussaint, MD

"If the road seems all uphill at the moment, then get ready for the breathtaking view at the top."

~ Author Unknown

I originally thought I was heading toward a primrose path; instead, I found myself trying to climb a greasy pole. Despite concentrated planning and effort, I found myself repeatedly back at square one.

My early life was easy. I had gone to all-girl Catholic schools my entire life. I was a very good student, and I had no drama at home; the future seemed straightforward. School was easy and enjoyable. I did not anticipate failure or struggles could possibly lie ahead.

I started college as a pre-med student, satisfying my desire to also write by starting a magazine while going to school. My best friend Michele loved the idea, and we set out to pursue our big dream together. Never mind that we had no experience, did not have a penny to spare and that this plan would require twice as much time commitment as simply going to college. We charged forward, dividing the editing tasks and the important interviews between us. We built a team and started holding regular brainstorming meetings. We used all kind of strategies to avoid detection, because we knew that young people meeting to discuss issues (under the Duvalier government in Haiti) could raise suspicions.

One member of our team was a well-known journalist named Ezequiel, who had been invited by my friend Michele. He was an original character, a bit controversial. His light jokes and his classical music program on late radio belied his strong political beliefs. In addition to receiving sound advice, having a real member of the local press in our group had its perks, like going with him to real interviews.

It was the summer before medical school. The school system in Haiti followed the French program; two years of baccalaureate meant that we finished school after the 14th grade. Then it was straight to university, where there was a preparatory year. We were 18 years old and our heads were full of unrealistic projects, but we meant well.

Then came the wake-up call. An acquaintance met Michele and I and told us that Ezequiel had been arrested the night before, at the radio station, after his program of classical music. From the note he left behind, he obviously realized that he would not come back.

We had done nothing wrong, but that was not enough to feel safe under such circumstances. We hoped that his arrest was not related to our meetings, but we expected to be called any day for questioning. After all, we had met several times. We were worried, even scared, especially since we had not let our parents know about the project. In retrospect, we were completely out of touch with reality. That "calling for questioning" belonged to books and movies, not a dictatorship.

I was also waiting for the fallout. After all, this was a well-known journalist, from a major radio station. He was related to a prominent playwright. There would be noise and protest. The authorities would have some "splaining" to do. Right?

The real nightmare started a few weeks later, when nothing happened. No public outcry, not even a public acknowledgement of the event by the radio station. Someone well known had disappeared in plain view, without a trace, like a villain swallowed by quicksand in an old Hollywood movie — and there was no public reaction. I was initially shocked and befuddled; as the truth hit me, I then became really upset. Upset to see the real face of the dictatorship. Upset that we could have been so naïve, thinking that we could have changed the world, upset to have assumed some good faith on the part of the authorities.

And I was mad at my school and the nuns — the whole system. Sure, we were given the best education available. But we were unprepared for real life; we were not even aware of the environment in which we were growing up. At least I was not. The big dream had to be put on hold.

I became emotionally numb. I was experiencing post-traumatic stress disorder, but I did not know it. I was two years into medical school before I started feeling alive again. I did not have the maturity to learn the necessary lessons from the event, except that our relative political peace and stability had an ugly underside. I focused on my studies and the challenges ahead instead of thinking about the dark side of the world.

By the end of my residency training, another choice loomed large: where to go for specialization. It was not exactly a choice, but the result of hard work and sheer luck. Some graduates went directly into private practice in Port-au-Prince or back to their hometown. Others would obtain a scholarship and go to Europe, with their family's financial support.

The rest took a chance on the American examination, waited for the results in agony, applied for a position, and then waited some more — sometimes for years. Many accepted an opening in a specialty that was not their first choice because it was not prudent to be picky.

This is why I felt so lucky when I was granted direct admission as an exchange clinical trainee into a university fellowship program in hematology, my field of choice. Even though I had passed my exam, I had also just gone through a difficult personal time. I was coming out of a long-term relationship and my mother's health was failing. My family cocoon was gone.

This training position felt like a gift from God after the recent events. I had to leave my mother behind to build a new life, but she was supportive; she did not want me to miss the opportunity. I am an only child, and except for a cousin living miles away, we were the last two members of the family left in Haiti. Our extended family — widowed aunts, cousins with their spouses and children — was scattered all over North America: New York, Chicago, Boston and cities in Canada.

It was a bittersweet separation. I had to leave my mother at a nursing home. Granted, this was the very first in the country, built out of town on a large property with a brook, and my mother had expressed interest from the time she heard the ads on the radio. I left Haiti intending to return home after three years. This plan made it easier to go.

I was in the United States only six months when my mother unexpectedly passed away. The rug was pulled out from under me. I had no one to go back to, no anchor. I tended to the urgent task of making funeral arrangements from a distance, and through this I discovered my longing for a sister. I wished I had a sibling who could share my grief. We had never had a death in the family while I lived in Haiti. We did not have a family plot. Furthermore, my scattered family could not fly home before the end of the week.

In those days, hotels were mostly outside Port-au-Prince and typically too expensive for the locals. They were resorts, built for the tourist industry. Cellular phones did not yet exist, so every international communication involved calling someone waiting in a booth at the phone company.

I did well around the time of the funeral. I kept it together, managed everything and came back to work. I was functioning, just a bit sad. It was a cold September.

Two months later, my roommate had a baby on Thanksgiving Day via C-section. I spent long days at the hospital, supporting her. My roommate's husband, a resident in training at the same hospital, was busy day and night. For weeks, she was keeping house, caring for a two-year-old son and taking care of her newborn daughter, while recovering from her surgery. These were hard days.

Then, right before Christmas, I found her elated when I came home. Her mother was coming to visit for two weeks, to help her. I was happy for her. It was a needed relief. The following day, while attending a lecture at the hospital, I started hyperventilating and went into a full-blown nervous breakdown. It had dawned on me that my mother would *never* come to visit, whether I had a child or not.

At that point, all the loneliness and the stress of being in a different country and culture came crashing in on me. I was finally grieving. That was a hard holiday season.

Within two months, Duvalier had fled Haiti. There was euphoria and new hope in the streets of Little Haiti in Miami. Growing up, we often wished for justice to be exacted from the bad guys.

But now, despite the sense of relief, another reality dawned on me. The only regime I had known my entire life was gone, replaced by uncertainty. As changes began, families who never dared to discuss politics were now divided. I had no family home where to return. I had lost my anchor a second time.

I was physically in the US, but I had to be there emotionally and mentally. As part of the process, I had to transition from a visiting medical trainee to a US licensed physician. That meant getting into a residency program. Again. It took gut and resolve: I was in effect starting a medical training for the third time.

I reached a level of physical exhaustion I had never experienced before, putting in 36 to 40 hours every three days. I also underwent severe emotional turmoil; like a new swimmer afraid to let go of the pool's edge, I was clinging to memories of Haiti, unaware that the country I had known was changing, and fast. I was mentally living in a place that did not exist anymore. At the same time, I knew I had to integrate into the new culture that was my new future. I was in Miami in the heydays of boat people and the AIDS epidemic. People were not always nice.

However, as time passed, I noticed a subtle change. I was feeling better in my skin. I was a stranger in a foreign land, but the program was full of foreign graduates going through the same growing pains. There was comfort in shared misery and mutual support. Furthermore, my years taking care of cancer patients had shown me incredible human suffering, but also inspiring dignity and fortitude. I developed self-reliance and inner strength.

As time went on, I had to face many more challenges, both administrative and personal. I came across negative behavior like I had never seen before — false friendships, unbridled jealousy, sheer meanness and greed — both from my compatriots and locals. I saw aspects of my own culture I had never encountered back home. When this happened, I deliberately decided to focus on the good and the positive. For every disappointing encounter, I also built relationships with great mentors, friends and peers. Sometimes good and bad came from the same people.

Once my gruesome hospital schedule was over, I pursued some of my interests: arts, culture, volunteer work and philanthropy. I read to children in shelters, cleaned parks, painted schools with the United Way and mentored battered women through the Junior League. I was chosen to sit on the Miami Commission on the Status of Women. There, I had access to some public television spots, and created some education programs in Creole.

I was a finalist for the JC Penney Award for community work and received a congratulatory letter from the White House.

With another friend working for the Miami-Dade County Mayor, I helped create the Haitian Cultural Heritage Month, which has now become a countrywide event. I got to choose the month and the event; together we shaped its content as it is still celebrated today. I helped single mothers get access to business training through the Women's Business Development Center at IFU and mentored adolescents with the Future Women Business Leaders.

But above all, I gained inner strength and reached a new state of maturity. I learned to forge ahead despite challenges and difficulties. From my painful moments, I have learned empathy and forgiveness. I am able to provide heartfelt counseling to my depressed patients. From my experience in oncology, I am able to offer support to patients and their relatives facing end of life in the hospice setting. I have also gotten in touch with my own spirituality. Like the preacher said on TV, out of your pain can come your purpose.

Through all of these experiences, I have grown bold. There was no sharp demarcation between the time of challenges and the moment I started feeling free and happy. It was an inner shift that happened because of deliberate decisions to focus on the positive. Life is much richer that way.

It sounds like a cliché, but you fail only if you think that your challenges are insurmountable. Challenges are to be expected; they make you stronger. Life may test you, people may even try to harm you, but your fortitude is yours and only yours. Remember that the same carbon that makes up soot, when under enough pressure, becomes a diamond, strong, resilient, unique.

About the Author

Marie Rosy Toussaint, MD studied medicine in her native Haiti, and continued her training at the University of Miami Jackson Memorial Hospital. She currently practices in Central Florida. She is passionate about wellness, disease prevention and patient education. She adopts a holistic approach to medicine. Besides being an internist, she sees terminally ill patients and their families at a Hospice House. She is also a Wound Care Specialist.

In her free time, she enjoys reading, writing, movies, tennis, cooking, dancing, meditation and the Fine Arts. She lectures on wellness and women's health. She may be reached at Healthsource49@aol.com.

Chapter Fifteen

Dare The Impossible

By Victor Eke-Spiff

"Your dream is the life you love to live, the hero you love to become and the passion you love to express, that your purpose might be fulfilled – DARE TO DREAM."

~ Victor Eke-Spiff

The Webster dictionary defines "dare" as "to have adequate or sufficient courage for any purpose; to be bold or venturesome; not to be afraid; to venture …" and "impossible" as "not possible; incapable of being done of existing; unattainable in the nature of things, or by means at command; insuperably difficult under the circumstances; absurd or impracticable; not feasible…"

The mantra "dare the impossible" therefore infers that we can muster up adequate or sufficient courage to achieve that which is unattainable in the nature of things or by means at command.

Man has set foot on the moon, something once believed to be impossible. Today, I was able to send mail from here to the other side of the world in a few seconds. These and many more seemingly impossible dreams have been realized. As we continue to aim higher, many dreams that are being considered impossible today shall also be actualized in the future.

Thought leaders such as Brian Tracy and Mary Morrissey teach that each of us is different from all other human beings who have ever lived. They also categorize our innate and universal human desires into four segments: health and well-being, relationships, creative expression and financial freedom. Thanks to the instruction of these sage leaders, I periodically take a quick assessment of my desires and achievements in each of these areas. This simple exercise helps me to focus and to manage my life well.

Give this exercise a try. On a scale of one to ten, with one being the least satisfactory and ten being the most satisfactory, assess your satisfaction in each of these areas:

Health: We all desire to be mentally and physically healthy — to have a sound mind, be happy and enjoy every moment of life, free from the hurts and aches of the past as well as the anxieties of the future. We also want to be physically fit and energized so we can accomplish our daily tasks and achieve goals.

Love and Relationships: Everyone wants attention and care. We want to love freely and be loved in return, enjoying intimate personal and social relationships with people we love, like and respect, who love, like and respect us in turn.

Creative Expression: We all want to be able to feel and express our unique talents and abilities. We would like to be and do whatever we want to do, be inspired and live out our aspirations as we make choices and uphold values that help others and prove relevant.

Financial Freedom: We all would like to adequately meet our financial obligations and not feel restricted in the choice of places we can visit, the food we'd like to eat and the material things we want to buy.

When I perform this exercise, I write down one word that best describes my state of being in the moment and a word that best describes the way I'd like to feel. Usually the two words are opposite in meaning. For example, perhaps I have chronic pain in my back, and I'd like to be healthy and relieved of this pain. My notes in the Health category might read, "Pain; free-of-pain." I learned from my personal development training that there are two sides to every situation and that I can cultivate the habit of shifting from one point of feeling to the other in any situation. However, to realize these goals in actuality, I also plan ways to address disparities between how I feel in the moment and how I wish to feel. Then I do my best to faithfully follow the plans I have devised.

Hebrews 11: 3 states, "Because of our faith, we know that the world was made at God's command. We also know that what can be seen was made out of what cannot be seen."

In other words, everything in life is created twice. It starts with a thought in the mind before it manifests in our life experience. Thus, to actualize your dream, you must first conceive of the dream and nurture it in your mind. Your thoughts guide your words, which become your actions. Your actions become habits, which forms the foundation of your character and eventually becomes your lifestyle. As such, it is possible to start living out your dream by assuming in the moment the outcome you desire to actualize.

I also learned from positive mindset training that the mind responds to repetition and pictures. Repetition programs the mind to align with your dreams, enabling you to discover the necessary opportunities, events and situations that can make your dreams come true. The words we speak become our persuasion, and if directed in favor of what we dream about or seek, it will be as "a lamp unto our feet and the light unto our path" that leads us to self-fulfillment. Pictures refer to the images of your dream that you can see in your mind's eye. Furthermore, the mind creates in two ways — by design and by default. If you intentionally conceive an idea in the mind, then it is by design; but if the mind picks a random pattern from the past, then it is by default, which is unlikely to yield positive results for you if you have been negative in the past.

If you are unsure if you will benefit from positive mindset training, take note of your mindset as you evaluate the four areas of common human desires. Most people have a misgiving in one or more areas. If you are unsatisfied, then you might benefit from a coach or mentor in positive mindset training. I do this every day and have been edified by positive mindset training for over 20 years now.

The following quote by Brendon Burchard, CEO of High Performance Academy, describes why I love to share my story with others: "When we feel as though we are contributing to the world, we gain a profound sense of meaning and purpose."

I know that I am who I am today because of my strong desire to aim higher and become a better person. My mission in life is to be courageous, to live life purposefully, respect my loved ones, grow and strengthen and share my gifts so that I might help positively affect others to grow their lives and businesses. This is my passion.

Why People Don't Actualize Their Dreams

We start out dreaming big dreams, but as the years pass we get distracted by routines and obligations. We make mistakes; we run into obstacles. Soon we find ourselves carrying baggage from past poor decisions, wishing that our current circumstances were better. We allow discontentment to overtake us, and that mindset becomes our entire worldview. We look at life through discouraged glasses, discolored by regrets from the past. We forget that all things that happened in the past are now behind us. We live in the present, not in the past.

Another reason we get stuck and don't actualize our desires is we worry about things that might happen in the would-be tomorrow. But tomorrow is yet to come; we don't live there now. The fear of tomorrow is only an imagined threat of what might happen.

Many people leap back and forth between frustrations of the past and worries about the future. To make this worse, they also limit themselves through self-sabotaging self-talk, saying things like:

"I can't do this."

"It's too hard."

"Not at my age."

"No one can do this."

Many people believe they don't have the right connections, education or finances. Others cast blame upon fate or the people surrounding them. These negative attitudes become self-fulfilling prophecies, limiting chances of finding success.

My Story

In my many years of service with an oil company, I spent a good amount of time as a laboratory man. Although I was very familiar with the layout of each of the plants, I never worked as a process man. As is common all over the world, when things go well with process, the direct operations people are commended (with no praise given to those in the lab), but when problems arise, they blame the service — the laboratory people.

One day, the plant manager informed me that I would be required at the floating production, storage and offloading location of a sister company offshore. He told me that the plant had been under intensive stress because of fouling problems for the past eleven months. "We want you to go and help them out of the problem," he said. Then he added, "Experts have been flown in on five different occasions for this problem, and yet the problem still persists."

Fear gripped me. How could I solve a problem that five experts could not solve? One of them even said they would have to do a partial plant facility modification. What did I know beyond what these renowned experts knew? I was not even familiar with this particular process facility!

I was afraid. What if something worse happened after my visit or as a direct result to action I suggested? I worried constantly. The day before I was to go offshore, I asked to see the manager. Apparently he knew I wanted to be relieved of the assignment, so he avoided me. He had told me earlier before, "This is an opportunity for you. I don't know why I am doing this, sticking out my neck for you. Let me know if you need anything to succeed in this assignment." That night I decided to simply do my best and trust that it would all work out, and I slept like a baby.

I landed on the platform offshore the following morning and feeling surprisingly confident. As I met the guys on board, I saw that they were warm and friendly. They walked me through their plant facility and answered all my questions. We examined fluid samples at different points, and I spotted where the problem was coming from: a cocktail of incompatible chemicals they were injecting into the system. I requested they stop all chemical injections and let the plant adjust itself. Four hours later, the process regained proper operation. My manager was on top of the world, and everybody else was happy, too. And me? I got an excellent raise.

As you can see, assuming a positive mindset can open doors to opportunities.

Activation Points

In addition to the positive mindset lessons I have described thus far, I have also learned a very useful way to test potential dreams you may be exploring. Honestly answer the following questions:

- In each area of life, does your dream enliven you?
- Is it worthy of you?
- Does it fit with your core values?
- Does it require you to grow?
- Does it scare you and inspire you to learn something new?
- Will it positively impact others?

If the answer to all six questions is yes, then it is most likely a good dream for you. If not, you might have to keep redefining your dream in that area until it scores a "yes" to all the questions.

I encourage you to also ask yourself, "Why do I want it to happen?" instead of, "How can I make it happen?" By focusing on the "why," you will increase your passion and the deep driving desire that will cause extraordinary things to begin to happen. Then articulate your dream, expressing gratitude and envisioning the fulfillment of your dream. If you do this, the "hows" will fall into place: ideas, resources, people, opportunities, etc.

Note of caution: Whenever you get stuck on the "how," be sure to return your focus to the "why." Stay open to solutions and opportunities. Options will appear, sometimes in the form of a conversation, an article or piece of advice you hear from a friend or colleague. You will be amazed at the results!

Dream On
We all have dreams. Embrace your dreams, realizing that you will impact other people as you pursue actualization of your dream. Do so with positive intent, influencing others as you find fulfillment.

Dream on. There is no better time than now.

About the Author

Victor Eke-Spiff is a Life coach, speaker and writer. He helps people to realize their wealth of mind, so that they can live a life of meaning and purpose.

Victor is a certified dream builder coach. He has been seen on stage with Mary Morrissey, CEO of Life Mastery Institute, featured in USA Today, Wall Street Today, and the United Nations. He is a published author of the book titled, *Success Manifesto* and producer of the film, *The Brian Tracy Story – Maximum Achievement.*

Victor continues to participate in trainings and programs with top motivational speakers and success coaches of our time.

Victor Eke-Spiff loves playing the piano. He and his beloved wife, Edibau reside in Port-Harcourt, Nigeria with their three sons and one daughter.

Contact Victor:

Telephone: +234 806 949 6081

Email: victorekespiff@yahoo.com

Website: www.myvitorio.com

Chapter Sixteen

I've Met An Angel

By Doug Evans

"If you had not fallen
Then I would not have found you
Angel flying to close to the ground
And I patched up your broken wing…"

~ Willie Nelson

Have you ever met an angel? I know I have. I even know that I've met more than one, but I want to tell you about one special one. Willie Nelson once wrote a song about angels flying too close to the ground. I believe that angels can never get too close; they are needed today more than ever.

Cathy LaBash and her husband Chuck own the Chocolate Gallery Café in Warren, Michigan. They have been friends of mine for over twelve years. If you stop by on a Sunday morning, you will likely find me and my wife Mary Ann having breakfast with Cathy. When you visit the café, Cathy will smile at you like she's known you forever. She'll give you a hug, even if you are a first time customer. You will feel her warmth, but the roots of all those smiles are some really tough times and an inspiring story.

Cathy has faced situations that would cause the average person just to give up and toss in the towel. She has indeed taken rests at times, but she always presses on, and she improves the lives of those around her as she does so.

She has lived through way too many cancer stories, many more than anyone should ever have to. If you've ever watched a close family member or friend battle cancer, you know what I mean. If you haven't experienced this, you're lucky. Statistics say one day you will.

Cathy lost her father to cancer and then her mother from complications caused by cancer. At an early age, she was devastated by this evil disease.

In high school a friend was diagnosed with cancer, and then passed away shortly after graduation.

Then, a close co-worker in her mid-twenties suddenly died right before her eyes. A medical black cloud seemed to follow Cathy every day.

A few years after these losses, other major life challenges upset her day-to-day life. Life would never be the same. Cathy was very depressed, confused and lost for a long time. It took almost two years before there was any sign or even a slight improvement in her life.

Then one day, Cathy was invited at work to listen to Michael Wickett, a motivational speaker. Now, I've worked with Michael over the years and I've heard him speak many times. He is a very good presenter. He is very upbeat and inspiring. The words Michael spoke that day touched her wounded heart. They penetrated the tough shell she had developed and opened her heart to a glimmer of hope. She had been searching, but not finding, and now Michael's words launched the discovery of a new world for Cathy, the world of self-improvement.

After this introduction to self-improvement, Cathy searched very hard for more and more knowledge about this new world. She found Wayne Dyer books at her local library. She adopted his message of optimism and his reinforcement of the power of God. She especially fell in love with the line, "If you know who walks beside you at all times on the path that you have chosen, you can never experience fear or doubt again."

This quote would become Cathy's mantra in the years ahead.

Cathy was in the process of mending the broken pieces in her life when suddenly one of her closest friends was diagnosed with breast cancer.

Cathy helped her friend throughout her struggles, but in the end, her friend passed away. The death of her friend triggered many terrible memories, yet Cathy pushed on. She relied on her faith in God for another five years or so, and then the unimaginable happened. Cathy was diagnosed with lobular breast cancer in her right breast.

Because of her family history, Cathy had been tested and told by doctors that she was fine many times, but Cathy kept hearing God telling her to get more tests done. She never expected the shocking news she received. Yet this little voice kept talking to her, even after the cancer was found in her right breast. Eight weeks after the first diagnosis, ductal cancer was also found in her left breast. Fear, confusion, insecurity and grief ensued. Surgery and chemotherapy followed. Misery moved in. Cathy had watched her dear friend lose the battle, and the memories haunted her.

Cathy's husband, Chuck struggled to remain positive and supportive. Times were very, very tough. They prayed fervently, day and night. On top of Cathy's illness, Chuck and Cathy had yet more stress: a new small restaurant to run. Chuck was the head chef and Cathy was the general manager of their restaurant. With this new battle with Cathy's cancer, they just couldn't devote the time necessary to the restaurant, so they had to close it down. Maybe permanently. Their dream business was gone, as was their sole source of income.

Thanks to God, Cathy recovered. It was a slow and exhausting journey, but she made it. Life settled down once again; they reminded themselves that God is good. They reopened the restaurant and relished a time of peace and prosperity.

Seven years passed and then life got messy again, as it often does. The year started with a black cloud chasing Chuck. It was his turn.

Early in the year, Chuck was struck by a bicycle. A student was running late for school, traveling very fast, and ran into Chuck as he left a storefront. His elbow was broken and he became the one-armed cook cartoonists might poke fun at. Shortly after this, he was repairing his roof at his Northern Michigan cabin when he fell through the roof and had to be airlifted to a regional hospital for head injuries and a pretty nasty concussion. Then, as if that wasn't enough, later that same year, major back surgery was required. Another curve ball tossed into the lives of the LaBash family.

Due to all these injuries, Chuck was not able to work at the café as much as he wanted to. It was Cathy's turn to lend support, taking her away from the café as well. A strong staff pitched in and kept them in the game. The poor economy of the metro Detroit area had already affected sales and profits, and now there were even more obstacles. Still, they made it through the year... or so they thought.

Thanksgiving arrived. Cathy was working on her computer when she started to experience stabbing pains in her side. God spoke to her again, telling her she must be tested for these pains. She was pretty sure it wasn't cancer because with the surgery, treatment regiment, and maintenance program she had completed, there was less than a three percent chance of cancer ever coming back. She wondered and worried about what it could be.

But after careful testing, it was determined that yes, against the odds, the ductal cancer was back, but this time in the lymph nodes. Chemo started all over again and this time radiation, too. Worry and doubt returned. Chuck and Cathy were terrified. Time passed and prayers were answered.

Over the years Wayne Dyer himself befriended Cathy and Chuck and began stopping by the restaurant for breakfast whenever he was in town. Wayne was also no stranger to cancer; he himself had been diagnosed with leukemia, and as he walked out on stage during his last visit to Detroit, he had spoken the words, "I am well." Cathy was moved by these words and memorized them quickly. This became her new mantra.

With these words and more prayers, once again cancer was defeated and no longer part of Cathy's life. She had now beaten and conquered cancer three times, but in 2014, four years later, the damnable cancer returned again.

If anyone else felt like quitting, it was Cathy at this moment in her life. Pause for just a second and imagine what she felt at this time. Think of Chuck. Her family. Think of the odds, the discouragement and the weariness. They were exhausted. Worn out.

But Cathy fought on, this time, choosing chemo and a holistic approach to destroying the cancer cells threatening her life. To do this wisely, Cathy dove into researching, seeking out the most proven holistic and natural ways to defeat cancer. She changed her diet, began drinking teas that could fight cancer, and started using essential oils.

But not only did she adopt a new lifestyle just to save herself. She decided to share her newfound knowledge with anyone who might need it. The research invigorated her, and she chose to trust that God was using her to inspire others as she fought the battle. This was the start of Cathy evolving into an angel.

She defeated cancer for the fourth time, and as an angel-on-earth Cathy decided to share her secrets with others.

She thought about her battles and identified the key factors to her victory. Prayers, love and support had strengthened her. Knowing a friend was praying for her, receiving a phone call, spending time with a friend for a short visit — all of these things helped her stay strong enough to fight until she found health again.

You may not know this, but angels (by definition) are divine messengers of God. In my book *A Leprechaun in your Pocket,* I talk about guardian angels. Guardian angels are very important to the Irish and should be important to all of us. Guardian angels play an important role in Christianity. They exist to protect, guide and care for others. They relay to us "nudges from God." They show us how to embrace faith and how to chase away and combat fear.

Today if you stop by Cathy's restaurant you'll see her quietly visiting with guests, and discretely sharing her knowledge to help others fight and conquer illnesses, especially cancer. Cathy glides from table to table, reassuring, educating and inspiring anyone who will accept her help. She seeks to help the people drawn into her circle of light; she pursues every possible opportunity to ease the pain, frustration and fear she knows all too well. She will answer any question. If by chance she doesn't know the answer, she will find it.

Most customers have no idea what she has gone through, or what all the quiet conversations they observe are all about. But God knows what they're about. I know what they're about. And now you know, too.

The country group Alabama in their song, "Angels Among Us," tells us about people like Cathy LaBash in these lyrics: "I believe there are angels among us, sent down to us from somewhere up above. They come to you and me in our darkest hour, to show us how to live."

Yes, angels are here to show us how to live, angels like Cathy. Cathy will help many more people, and show them how to live a life when they are fighting cancer.

If you are in a dark hour, look for an angel. If you have lived through difficult times, share the lessons you have learned with others. You may get tired, and you may need to rest and rely on the strength provided by an angel for a while, but when you conquer and defeat the struggles you faced, it is your turn to give hope and love to the people you meet.

About the Author

Doug Evans (doug@discoveryourmissingpower.com) is an accomplished executive coach, corporate trainer, author, speaker, writing consultant, CPA and founder of several inspirational personal development sites on the Internet, including www.discoveryourmissingpower.com. Doug is an expert in masterminding with individuals or groups. His process can help you discover solutions to challenges you are facing and produce more money, more time and more smiles which will, reignite your passion in daily living.

Chapter Seventeen

From Buying Groceries On A Chevron Card To Running Jim Rohn International

By Kyle Wilson

"I find it is easier to go ahead and become successful than it is to spend all your time making excuses."

~ Jim Rohn

It was 1987 when I made the decision to leave Vernon, Texas, a town of 11,000 people and the birthplace of my first business, a small car detail shop. I started the business at the age of 19. By the time I hit 24, I owned and ran the service station and employed ten people.

But I had a feeling that there was something more out there for me. When I turned 26, I decided to sell my business and move to the big city about three hours away — Dallas, Texas. Little did I know that within five years, I would be running Jim Rohn International.

Keep in mind, I never went to college. I never even had a mentor. I found my way on my own, and you can, too.

At first I stayed inside my comfort zone; I opened another detail shop. However, an opportunity soon presented itself, and I accepted a sales job that included travel, perks and paid pretty well. It was a satisfying job, but within a year I found myself missing the entrepreneurial journey. I felt I was meant to do something more significant with my career.

One day I got a call that changed my life. I was told by my employer that when they hired me they had no idea that my driving record was as bad as it was, and that their insurance company would not cover me. A substantial piece of the job was travel; I drove approximately 1,000 miles a week. I took a series of driving courses, but then I was in a very minor car accident. That ended my sales career with that company.

Naturally, I had to find a job. I considered starting my own business again, but someone suggested I get a job at a high-end car dealership. I had a strong sense that this was the right thing to do; intuitively, I felt sure this was an opportunity I needed to explore.

Sure enough, I got hired, went through the required training and then started on the floor. One of the new guys sold three cars his first day. Me? Nothing. A goose egg. On the second day, we kicked the morning off with a sales meeting presented by a guest speaker, Jerry Haines, who lectured about personal development and success. At the end of his talk, I reserved a ticket to his upcoming seminar. I wasn't sure if I could get off work, but Jerry gave me a ticket anyway and offered to let me pay for it after I'd had a chance to talk it over with my boss. After the meeting, I returned to the floor and ended my second day on the job with yet another goose egg in sales.

Monday rolled around. I went in to work and put on my best face, but after an hour, I quit. I will never forget the conversation with my wife at lunch that day. I told her, with complete confidence, that I knew I was supposed to work there *and* I knew I was supposed to quit that day. As you can imagine, that didn't go over too well.

With all the stress about the job, I had totally forgotten that I had committed to go to the seminar until Jerry called me. I told him that I wasn't certain I needed to go the seminar because I was no longer working in sales. He assured me it would be a great investment, and in fact asked me if I would be interested in becoming a sales rep for him. We set up a time to discuss the possibility after the seminar.

A few weeks later, I attended the seminar and met with Jerry. He gave me an opportunity to promote two speakers, Dan McBride and Ken Lutz.

A few months later, Jerry gave me a cassette tape and said, "Listen to this. The speaker is Jim Rohn; he's my mentor. He also mentors Dan, Ken and a young-and-upcoming speaker Tony Robbins. I may need help promoting Jim in the future, and I'd like you to check out his philosophy."

I was blown away by Jim's message; I told Jerry I was 100 percent committed. I would love to promote and represent this man.

Within a few months I was doing exactly that, and over the next two years I put on at least twelve seminars in the Dallas, Fort Worth, Houston and San Antonio areas. It was an amazing experience.

Now, while I loved the job and quickly became Jerry's top salesperson, I didn't make very much money. I was barely getting by; in fact, I was going into debt.

I resolved to go out on my own and to change the model. Instead of getting 300 to 400 people in a room for multiple events in the same city and promoting the same speaker every 60 days, I wanted to get at least 2000 people in a room and do only four events a year (instead of six). It was an intimidating goal, so I came up with a plan that I felt matched the goal.

I decided I had to promote to a large market every three months and feature at least two world-class speakers. I settled on Atlanta, Georgia as my first target market. After my final Jim Rohn seminar in Austin, my wife and I packed up the U-Haul and made the trip to Atlanta to start a new company so I could go out on my own.

Our first big challenge was the fact that we had no money. My American Express and Visa were both maxed, and I was about to put on a seminar that required capital.

I'll never forget arriving in Atlanta and searching for a Chevron convenient store that sold bread and bologna (in addition to gas) so I could buy food with my Chevron credit card.

Next big challenge: where were we going to stay? Immediately I negotiated with one of the major hotels in downtown Atlanta, convincing them to exchange tickets for their sales team to attend the event for five days lodging in the hotel. This enabled me to stay in the hotel, hammer the phones to book sales meetings. Serendipitously enough, they agreed to this arrangement.

Time was of the essence. I spent the following five days pounding the pavement, booking appointments with companies to speak and selling tickets to the event. I also secured two speakers — Brian Tracy and Og Mandino. I had never worked with them before, and they both required deposits. I explained that I was in the middle of a move and would send their deposits the following week. Of course, I wanted to book Jim Rohn, but Jerry (understandably) wasn't happy with me leaving, so that was not an option.

I immediately started on the phones, cranking out calls from the hotel. What did I do when the hotel told me I had racked up a hundred-dollar phone bill that first day and asked me to settle up? I negotiated unlimited phone calls for another ticket to the event. To my good fortune, they said yes.

In addition to booking myself to speak to companies, I also had to find us a place to live. I found a corporate apartment that was completely furnished. It wasn't cheap, but was in a fantastic location, and they agreed to rent it to me for 50 percent cash and 50 percent in trade for tickets to the event. Once again, I didn't have the 50 percent in cash, but through the principles of *My Mammie Wants Her 50 Cents* from *Think and Grow Rich*, I was able to negotiate to pay the 50 percent trade in tickets right away and to pay the other 50 percent in cash in 30 days.

Before you know it, I had multiple talks booked. I didn't have tickets or brochures printed yet, but I had a date and I had speakers and I had a presentation. I had motivation, and motivation goes a long way. In my first corporate presentation I sold eight of the nine people tickets for the event (which was happening in nine weeks). When they asked to pay with a credit card, I said, "Guys, I'm not set up yet. I will be soon, but if you can write a check to me personally or pay cash, I will mail you your tickets once they are printed." Again, through serendipity or whatever you want to call it, all eight agreed to pay through cash or check.

Fast forward to nine weeks later. The event happened, as planned, and it was incredible. We had over 1300 people in attendance.

Next city? Chicago. This time, I wanted to work with Jim Rohn.

I humbled myself and spoke to Jerry, asking for permission to book Jim Rohn through him. Although Jim's fee was usually $4000, Jerry said I could book Jim, but the fee would be $10,000, and I would also have to buy X amount of product to sell at the event. He also insisted that I pay cash for the whole deal. I did it.

In Chicago, I promoted Og Mandino and Jim Rohn, and we had 1800 people attend the event. Next, we hit Washington DC (again with Og and Jim), and we had 2100 people. Then I promoted Jim Rohn and Brian Tracy in Sacramento, and we had 2600 people.

There were a few other cities along the way, and at some point in time Jerry and Jim had a parting of the ways. The business model Jerry had just wasn't working; he was deep in financial debt to Jim because his events were losing money.

I was in Kansas City doing a Jim Rohn/Brian Tracy event, when Jim informed me of this. I jumped on the opportunity, offering to represent and promote Jim. Jerry was my original mentor, and I did not want to do anything that would not be ethical, but Jim assured me that the partnership with Jerry was over. The debt was just too large.

We drew up a business plan and agreed with a handshake. That first year, I took Jim from 20 dates at $4000 apiece to 110 dates at $10,000 apiece, and that was the launch of Jim Rohn International.

A few years later I also launched YourSuccessStore.com. Between YSS and JRI, I was able to create 100+ products, build a million+ email list and start agenting for many other speakers and ventures. That partnership with Jim will forever be one of the great honors of my life. I am honored to have had the opportunity to work with the man who so changed my life.

My work with Jim began in 1990 (promoting him in Dallas). We started Jim Rohn International in 1993. Eventually, we sold all my companies in 2007, including Jim Rohn International. They were my companies; that was part of what made it work. Up until we began working together, Jim lost a great deal of money. Even Adventures in Achievement, which peaked in value at $800,000, had to be shut down due to money issues.

Why did it work? I spent my own money and paid Jim a percentage of every speaking date, every product we created and everything we did, whether it was profitable or not. That way Jim always got paid. This arrangement protected Jim and motivated me to do whatever it took to be successful.

It also empowered me to put on my marketing hat and aggressively build. That first year I came up with an idea called the *Excerpts From The Treasury of Quotes,* a viral marketing tool that sold over 6 million pieces. I then created similar products for Brian Tracy, Denis Waitley, Zig Ziglar, Mark Victor Hansen and others. The success of these projects enabled me to quickly create other products and to launch side ventures like Your

Success Store, where I was able to work with other speakers and cross-pollinate our products, lists and events.

In 2007, Stuart Johnson (who was in the process of buying *Success Magazine*) made a hard run to buy my companies over an 18-month period of time. Eventually, my team and I (we were now at 20 employees) decided to sell. I had an aggressive profit-sharing program, so the team was on board.

Sadly, Jim passed away approximately two years later. However, he made an impact while he was here, and I was fortunate enough to have worked with him and learned from him.

Jim, one more time, thank you for your friendship and mentorship in my life. I am forever honored and blessed! I will continue to share your message as long as I am able.

With love,

Kyle

About the Author

Kyle Wilson is a highly successful entrepreneur. He is the founder of Jim Rohn International, YourSuccessStore.com and The Lessons From Network and has collaborated with the top names in the personal development industry including, Jim Rohn, Og Mandino, Brian Tracy, Zig Ziglar, Les Brown, Denis Waitley, Darren Hardy and many others.

Kyle has filled hundreds of personal development events, launched and published over a dozen personal development publications reaching over a million subscribers a week and has produced/published over 100+ hours of DVD & CD programs and has sold millions of books through his publishing companies.

Kyle is the author of *52 Lessons I Learned from Jim Rohn and Other Great Legends I Promoted!* and co-authored *Chicken Soup for the Entrepreneur's Soul* with Mark Victor Hansen and Jack Canfield.

Connect with Kyle at www.KyleWilson.com/Connect

Email: kyle@kylewilson.com

Twitter: kwmarketing

IG: kwjimrohn

SC: kwjimrohn

Chapter Eighteen

What to Do Now

By Vic Johnson

Now that you know the difference between taking a break and giving up, what is the dream you want to achieve?

Think about this very carefully.

After all, what you work on today will eventually become your destiny. And while you can't build a pyramid overnight, you do have to decide which bricks to lay *today*. Eventually, the small actions you take — those bricks you lay — will become the foundation for your future life. And that's true whether you're starting at 18 or 80. It's never too late to start laying the foundation for what you want out of your life.

But you do have to make that decision as soon as possible, because it's time to get to work.

What you really have to find is a dream that's energizing enough that you'll feel motivated to begin the journey. And yes, there will be tough times during which you'll feel like quitting no matter how certain you are of success. But there will always be a way to get through. As the poet Robert Frost said, the best way out — is through.

In other words, the best way "out" of your current problems and challenges isn't to avoid them. It's to tackle them head-on with the kind of determination and persistence you read about throughout this book.

The best way "out" of your current situation isn't to try something else and hope it sticks. It's to determine where you want to go, what it will take to get there and start building your new empire today — brick by brick.

All You Need to Do Is Not Quit

It might sound silly. All you need to do is not quit. But consider the ramifications of this statement when you're at your worst.

You see, it's often our emotions that get the best of us. We might feel fine training for a marathon. But when it comes to mile 19 and you feel that you have absolutely nothing left to give, your brain will start to find the excuses that shut you down completely.

Maybe it will say, "You've accomplished a lot. If you quit right now, no one will blame you."

Maybe it will say, "Nineteen miles is enough to feel proud of."

Maybe it will say, "You need water. If you quit now, you can get some."

Your emotions will try and derail you. What you need to remember is that determination is a decision you make independent of your emotions. Determination is that choice you made back when you originally said, "I'm going to achieve this, no matter what happens."

No matter *what* happens. No matter *what* gets in your way. Even if what's getting in your way… is you.

All you need to do in that moment is not quit.

If you say, "Yeah, I can get some water," but your feet keep moving toward the finish line, that's a victory.

If you say, "Nineteen miles is a lot to be proud of, but twenty would better," that's a victory.

Persistence has magical results, but in its application, it's actually very simple.

All that's required of you is that you don't quit.

When In Doubt, Take a Break — But Don't Quit

Most of the time, when that little voice in your head says "Quit!" it's only to get you to stop temporarily. Maybe it wants you to take a break from running. Maybe it wants to you take on less stress at work. Whatever it is, you can often satiate this voice by taking a break temporarily.

But quitting? That's another story entirely.

Quitting is abandonment. Quitting is saying, "I'm done with this."

Taking a break, on the other hand, is not abandonment. Taking a break is saying, "I'll rest now, but I'll be back later."

As long as you're moving forward on a regular basis, you have every right to take a break once in a while. You have every right to make the journey as pleasurable and painless as possible. You shouldn't seek out pain when you can move toward your goal in other ways.

But there's also a very fine — and very real — line between taking a break and calling it quits.

In order to ensure that your breaks don't turn into abandoning your dream, make sure that you stick to your goals consistently. Heck, go to the gym for *five minutes* if it keeps your habit alive.

Don't let your goals die quietly. Don't let your dreams pass into abandonment simply because you don't have the energy to visit them every once in a while.

Take a break when you work too hard — but don't take a break when you work too little. Once you find the balance, you'll find the way to persistence that sticks.

Daily Exercises

Of course, cultivating a value like persistence doesn't happen overnight, either. You're going to want to cultivate the idea of persistence in the face of overwhelming opposition. And you can do that with a few daily exercises:

- **Affirmations.** Simply repeating, "I, [your name], am a famous novelist on [Date]!" is a great way to get energized. But you might want to consider adding a part about your persistence if you struggle in that department. If you have the discipline to invest time to articulate or document affirmations every single day, then it shows that you really do value the journey you're on.

- **Cold showers.** They sound crazy. Why take an uncomfortable cold shower when there's plenty of warm water to be had? Some self-discipline experts say it's the best way to build up your immunity to stress. Tony Robbins starts every day at home with a plunge in a 57-degree cold Jacuzzi that he says helps him get ready for an outstanding day. If you can handle a cold blast of water in the morning for no good reason other than your own self-discipline, then you'll train your emotions to handle obstacles on the path to your journey. Try it for 21 days and see if your life doesn't benefit.

- **Exercise.** There's no exercise like physical exercise. If you want to train yourself for endurance *and* persistence, then there's only one way: the challenge of the great outdoors. If you want to build up your persistence muscles, then you have to use them — literally. Climb that hill. Hike that mountain. Bike that path. Do what it takes to push yourself in your exercise and you'll build the ability to do so when it comes to your dreams as well.

Action Steps

Now that you've had a chance to absorb the lessons in this book, it's time to make them concrete. Let's take a look at your dreams and ask yourself how you can begin to make them a reality.

1. **Start with the end in mind.** Determine the finish line. For example, if you're going to run a marathon, then select a race six months from now that you can adequately train for. Give yourself adequate time, but make sure that you do ultimately pick a solid target. This will help keep you on the right course even when you feel like quitting.

2. **Create a system for achieving your goal.** It's not enough to have a goal. Now you have to think about the day-in, day-out work required to achieve it. If your goal is to get a promotion at work, then you know what your end game is. But what can you do *today* to achieve that goal? Create a *system* of "one extra piece of work every single day" that will empower you to give more to your employer than you get in return. This habit will ultimately lead the way forward to a promotion.

3. **Reward yourself for persisting.** Did you stick to your habit for seven days this week? Now's the time to reward yourself. Don't deprive yourself throughout the journey; you want to associate positive rewards with the work you've been doing. You'd be surprised at how much of a Pavlovian response you can cultivate within yourself, even when you're the one doing the rewarding.

4. **Look over your plans on a regular basis.** Let's say you had a goal to run a marathon in six months. After six weeks, maybe you look at how close you are to your goal and adjust your daily system. Do you need to run more? Get more sleep? Do you need to change your diet? Make adjustments as you go, because it's very difficult to get the plan right from the outset. Keep adjusting.

5. **Follow through until the end.** Eventually, it will come down to your desire for your goal and your grit. Make a vow to yourself now and write it down; you *will* achieve your goal.

Persistence isn't something that happens overnight — and neither are the dreams you want to achieve *with* this powerful tool.

Be patient. You'll learn that you can't do as much in a day as you once thought, but over time, as days become weeks and months and years, you will discover that you *do* have much more power to change the world then you ever could have imagined. So long as you keep laying those bricks, eventually, a pyramid will stand.

Other Books by Vic Johnson

Day by Day with James Allen

How To Write A Book This Weekend, Even If You Flunked English Like I Did

Goal Setting: 13 Secrets of World Class Achievers

It's Never Too Late And You're Never Too Old: 50 People Who Found Success After 50

52 Mondays: The One Year Path To Outrageous Success & Lifelong Happiness

The Magic of Believing: Believe in Yourself and The Universe Is Forced to Believe In You

Failure Is Never Final: How To Bounce Back Big From Any Defeat

Self Help Books: The 101 Best Personal Development Books

How I Created a Six Figure Income Giving Away a Dead Guy's Book

50 Lessons I Learned From The World's #1 Goal Achiever

How To Make Extra Money: 100 Perfect Businesses for Part-Time and Retirement Income

You Become What You Think About